# MOVING
## ON FROM
# TEACHING

# MOVING
## ON FROM
# TEACHING

*Career Development*
*For Teachers*

**Caroline Elton**

Kogan
Page

First published in Great Britain in 1987
by Kogan Page Limited, 120 Pentonville Road,
London N1 9JN

**British Library Cataloguing in Publication Data**

Elton, Caroline
  Moving on from teaching.
  1. Career changes—Great Britain
  I. Title
  331.7'02'0941    HF5384

  ISBN 1-85091-286-6

Printed and bound in Great Britain by
Biddles Ltd, Guildford

# Contents

# Acknowledgements

First and foremost I must thank Anne Miller. A chance encounter on the back of a jeep in the Sinai desert led to this book. I discovered that she was an ex-teacher who had written a very successful book for the American market on how to leave the teaching profession. Having left teaching two months previously in order to retrain as a psychologist, I would dearly have appreciated a good careers manual. So, I decided to build on Anne's original idea by writing this book for British teachers.

My thanks to Steven Briggs for his encouragement. Pat Pearce of the Polytechnic of Central London's Careers Advisory Service and Sally Hirst of Oxford University Appointments Committee were both driven mad by my frequent phone calls; the book has greatly benefited from the generous way they shared their expertise with me. John Wilson, the education adviser at the British Institute of Management, and Diane Dewar, the employment information services librarian at Holborn Library, both gave me enormous help and assistance. John Towers put considerable effort into the section on pensions. Anthony and Judith Julius, Suzanne Franks, Gabrielle Rifkind and Jonathan Levy directed me to the many happy and successful ex-teachers whom I interviewed for this book. Judith Campbell, Elaine Gordon and Jane MacFarlane deserve a special mention. Marcia and Miles Elton and Jill and Norman Franklin provided frequent baby-sitting, without which I would still be writing the first chapter, and I am particularly grateful to Jill Franklin for her constructive comments and to Miles Elton for his help with the Index.

Finally, I would like to thank Andrew Franklin who pushed me into writing this book, escaped to the States while it was being written, and then returned four days before it was finished, to help me tie up all the loose ends.

# Chapter 1
# Introduction

**The aim of this book**

The aim of this book is to provide practical careers advice to teachers who are considering leaving the profession. If you are a teacher contemplating a career change you are in good company. A 1985 survey found that over 15 per cent of the teachers who left at the end of the summer term were going into jobs *other* than teaching.

Happily there are many excellent and committed teachers who love their work, finding it both stimulating and fulfilling. These teachers do not need to think about changing their career. But, particularly given the current state of despondency in the profession, there are many others who experience much less satisfaction. This book is intended for them.

The basic premise is *not* that the only solution is to leave your job. Instead, it is the notion that you must analyse what you want to get out of your work, and ask yourself whether teaching is meeting these criteria. If there is a gap, then the book will show you the best ways of successfully changing careers.

You may discover that your feelings of dissatisfaction lie in your particular school, rather than in the profession itself, so you will seek another teaching appointment in a different school. Or perhaps you want to stay in teaching but will further develop a particular aspect of your work, to improve your prospects within the profession. If after reading the book you decide to stay in teaching, the book won't have failed. Far from it. You will know that you are working as a teacher, not because you can't think what else to do, but because teaching is what you *want* to do.

For some teachers the answer will be to leave the classroom but to stay within the educational field. Examples of this type of career change would be jobs in youth work, educational psychology or education in industry. With these no one will question the relevance of your teaching experience. In some cases (eg educational psychology) teaching is an essential prerequisite and you cannot do the job *unless* you have been a teacher. Moves of this kind, where you are leaving teaching but staying within 'education', are easier, as the change is seen in terms of career development rather than a career break.

But in this book you are shown that it is also possible to move into a field that has no obvious links with education. This is harder, and likely to take longer. You also have to contend with the fact that there is some mistrust of 'career changers'. However, if you use the book to guide you through the separate stages, you will be able to make a successful move into a career of your choice.

## Why are so many teachers changing their career?

I interviewed 50 teachers from both the primary and secondary sectors to find the answer to this question. The particular reasons why a teacher from the sample decided to change professions varied from individual to individual. But there were a few factors which were of critical importance and were cited by most of my interviewees. The following extracts from two secondary school teachers are typical:

> I became frustrated by the lack of opportunities and financial reward. There was also insufficient time and inadequate resources to do the job well.

> The major reasons underlying my decision to leave the profession were lack of prospects, deteriorating salaries, and disillusionment with government attitudes to education.

You might expect that these viewpoints were confined to Scale 1 teachers who had failed to gain promotion, but in fact they were found at all levels of the profession. The first quote was from a 27-year-old woman who in her four and a half years of teaching had worked as a head of year, in addition to having a scale point for responsibility within her department. She is now working as a training consultant in a computer software company. The second quote comes from a 33-year-old man who had taught for ten years and was a Scale 4 head of department. He now works as a sales consultant with a large insurance company.

Poor pay and promotion prospects, and lack of time and resources to do the job properly are cited by most of the ex-teachers. In addition, younger teachers often mention factors such as stress, problems with classroom discipline and inadequate support from senior management. Taken together it is clear that morale among teachers is at a low ebb. The problems in the profession which are making many teachers contemplate a career change are real rather than imaginary, and it is not surprising that many teachers are voting with their feet.

## How to go about changing career

There may be good reasons why many teachers are contemplating a career change, but listing some of the current problems in the profession does not provide an answer to the central question— *How does one go about leaving teaching?*

Clearly, you can just hand in your notice and then scan the classified ads in local and national newspapers, applying for any posts that sound interesting. That's all it takes to leave the profession. But if you want to choose a second career that is going to prove fulfilling, and you want to improve your chances of succeeding in this career, you need to plan your career change systematically. I'm not claiming that moving on from teaching is an *easy* process, only that it *is* possible.

## What this book provides

### 1. It is a book specifically for teachers

There are a number of general books on how to get a job, which can give you useful information about application forms, interviews etc. But this book is specifically for teachers who are considering changing their career.

In some respects a teacher who wants to change career is no different from any other career changer. Anybody in this situation is likely to face difficulties in working out what else they could do and finding out about opportunities that interest them. However, in other respects teachers are different. They are isolated within schools and they may have little experience or knowledge of careers outside education. Furthermore, some employers outside teaching have no idea about how demanding the teaching profession is. They don't realise the range of skills that you *have* to develop to survive in the classroom—skills such as effective public speaking, producing clearly written materials and organising your time to meet deadlines. If you analyse your teaching experience to extract the different skills that you have developed, you can present yourself to employers as an attractive candidate.

This book goes beyond general advice to consider how your background in teaching affects you at *each* stage in the career change process. For example, Chapter 3 (How to find out more about your next career) devotes considerable space to explaining ways in which you can approach and build up contacts in any field that interests you, even if the career has no obvious links with the teaching profession. In Chapter 5 (Interviews) there is a detailed section on how to respond when the interviewer challenges you about the relevance of your teaching background to the post on offer. The advice given throughout the book is based on the experience of more than 50 ex-teachers who have made successful moves out of the teaching profession.

## 2. It provides you with a framework

*Moving On From Teaching* guides you through the process of career change by giving you a structured framework. Successfully changing your job takes an enormous amount of time and effort. It's pointless applying for jobs in the newspapers that sound vaguely interesting if you haven't ascertained two things: first, that you *really* want to work in the field and second, given your background in teaching, that you have a remote chance of being considered for the post. Applying for jobs that are wrong for you or that you cannot get is a time-consuming and depressing business. You need to approach the whole process in a more systematic manner.

Changing career actually involves a series of distinct stages:

● Working out what your next career should be
● Finding out more about opportunities in your chosen field
● Writing application forms and CVs that will get you interviews
● Succeeding at interviews — getting the job

Inadequate planning at any of these stages can result in failure to find a fulfilling second career. For example, if you give insufficient thought to your career choice, you might land in a new job that you loathe. Alternatively, if you make a mess of the interview, then all the careful planning that has gone into the previous stages may be wasted. In order to help you plan, a separate chapter is devoted to each of these four stages.

If you follow through the stages outlined in the book, you will be approaching the process of career change in an organised, thorough manner. This won't *guarantee* you a job, but it will allow you to maximise your chances of finding a suitable alternative to teaching. Don't underestimate the importance of good organisation, or the amount of effort you will need to devote to the cause. This is what a former head of careers, now a BBC television producer, had to say on the matter:

If you are considering leaving teaching think very carefully about exactly what you are capable of doing, and set about your career change very systematically. A lot of people try to get out of teaching and a lot fail because they go about it fairly half-heartedly. I have been asked by countless teachers how I managed it, and the answer is I only did it after a longish slog and with considerable forethought.

## How to stick at it to the end

Careful planning of the different stages, and commitment, aren't the only important factors. It is also vital that you set yourself a *realistic* timetable for change.

You may have to cope with a number of rejected application forms, failed interviews and false starts before you finally settle yourself into your new career. As teachers, we get used to planning our working life according to ordered deadlines: We'll finish the unit on algebra by half-term, give the end of unit test, and then move on to percentages after the half-term break.

Changing your career isn't like this. You can't look in your diary and fix a date when your career plans will be finalised. The whole process is likely to take between six and twelve months, depending on what you want to do, and the amount of energy you put into it. So, do not set an unrealistic timetable, and then give up when your plans have failed to materialise within the allotted time.

Another aspect of weathering the inevitable disappointments is to make sure that you have a support network. If you decide to embark on a career change, there will be times when everything seems to be going wrong and you feel ready to pack it all in. When this happens, you need someone who will listen to you, as you pour out your worries and feelings of failure. It doesn't matter if this person is your partner, parent, or friend; the only important thing is that you have some sort of safety valve.

I wouldn't advise you to discuss your intentions too widely in the staffroom. Confide in a friend who is also a colleague, but don't make the ups and downs of your career plans a topic of general staffroom conversation. There are probably other people among the staff who would also like a change of career, but who lack the initiative or energy to do anything about it. If you tell everyone you talk to in the staffroom about your plans, and then your plans collapse, you are setting yourself up as a target for staffroom gossip and ridicule.

## How much does success depend upon luck?

You might think that the success of your career plans will depend largely on luck—whether the right job crops up in the right place at the right time. I would argue that there is no such thing as 'pure luck', and I like to use the American definition: 'Luck happens when preparation meets opportunity.'

The experience of an art teacher who moved into writing computer manuals illustrates the point. In the boom a few years ago, when all schools started getting microcomputers, no one in his school was qualified to teach computer studies. As he was interested in computer graphics and he had a flexible headmaster, the art teacher was encouraged to develop and teach a basic computer course. To prepare for the course he went into a major London bookstore to find a basic computing book for children, but as nothing suitable was available, he wrote his own. This teacher's background was in fine arts rather than computing, and his book was beautifully illustrated with his own cartoons. The book was so successful at school that his colleagues pushed him into trying to get it published, and he approached an acquaintance in the publishing field. This acquaintance wasn't much help until a publisher phoned her up a few weeks later and asked her if she knew anyone who could write a basic computing book for children. She put the publisher in touch with the art teacher, and not only was his book published, it sold 60 000 copies!

You could say it all boiled down to luck: if the publisher had not phoned the acquaintance to enquire about computing books, the deal would not have got under way. But that was the 'opportunity' part of the equation. In fact, the success rested on careful planning and preparation on the teacher's part: having the initiative to go into teaching computing to begin with; identifying a gap in the book market; writing his own book and then approaching a publishing contact. It's not really 'luck' at all.

## Should I really leave teaching?

Only *you* can answer this question. You know how much or how little satisfaction you are deriving from the profession and how much effort you would be willing to put into the process of changing your career. Leaving teaching is a serious step, and not one that should be taken lightly. But no one should go on and on doing a job that frustrates them. If you really are getting little fulfilment from teaching or, even worse, if you dread going into school every day, you should seriously consider a change.

There is a further point you should think about before you make a final irrevocable decision, and that is the 'grass is always greener outside teaching' fallacy. People outside the teaching profession have extremely inaccurate, stereotyped views of what working as a teacher is like, along the lines of:

> You don't do much... you finish around 3.30 and have all those nice long holidays. After a few years on the job you just recycle your lesson plans so you don't need to bother with lesson preparation.

The same is true for teachers, who may have equally mistaken ideas about jobs outside education: for instance, that publishing is one never-ending-expense-account lunch and that salaries are much higher than in teaching. Such fantasies are one reason why it is so important to plan your career change according to the framework given in the book. If you follow my advice, and you are considering a career in publishing, you will spend some time with a publisher or two, to find out what their jobs are really like. Furthermore, by the time you have worked your way through Chapter 2 (What should your next job be?) you should have built up a clear picture of what you are looking for in a job. When you actually go and meet your contacts you can find out if the job as they describe it is what you want.

Also remember that no job is perfect, and every one of the 3000 different occupational titles listed in the UK will have their boring aspects (although some are obviously drearier than others). As a teacher, it may be the marking or lesson preparation in the evening that gets you down the most. But every job has its equivalent.

## The first obstacle to overcome

There is an obstacle in the way of many teachers who are considering leaving the profession: the 'I'm just a teacher' syndrome. Sufferers from it say to themselves: 'I'll never find another job... I'm only a teacher.' The prognosis for finding a career alternative is not good if this syndrome is allowed to persist. Luckily a cure is available. Start analysing the different skills that you have developed in the course of your teaching career, and the symptoms will disappear.

The people in my sample who were 'just' teachers have managed to find themselves jobs across the whole careers spectrum: architect, publisher, computer programmer, TV producer, educational psychologist, art therapist, social worker, journalist, landscape gardener, research scientist, graphic designer, house-painter, actor, tax inspector, accountant, charity-administrator, to name only a few. But despite the variety of jobs that these people are now doing, they all agreed on one point—their present posts were nowhere near as demanding or tiring as their jobs in teaching.

*Chapter 2*

# What Should Your Next Job Be?

If you are thinking about leaving teaching the hardest decision will be working out what your next career should be. There is a great temptation to think of yourself as a failure—someone who is not making a satisfactory career out of teaching—and therefore someone who will be equally unfulfilled in their next job. Undoubtedly there will be times when you feel this way, but try to look on your decision to change from a more optimistic point of view.

The fact that you want to leave teaching does not mean that you will never find job satisfaction; teaching is a particularly difficult job. Many teachers leap into it with an idealised notion of what teaching will be like, based more on memories of their own school experience, than the reality of the contemporary classroom. Furthermore, despite the popular myth of the teacher whose working day finishes at 3.30, most teachers spend a considerable amount of time each evening and weekend preparing and marking work. Often teachers find that they are unable to go out at all during weekday evenings. The combination of these pressures with the demanding workload, relatively poor pay and low status, makes many teachers decide they want to leave the profession.

Even when you have decided that you want a career change, never regard the years you spent teaching as a waste of time. Whatever career you decide to pursue, the experience you have gained as a teacher will be invaluable. The range of skills that you have developed—public speaking, planning a programme of work, dealing sensitively with a large number of different people—can be applied to any career. The setting may change but you will not lose these transferable skills, so you have a considerable amount of expertise to offer a prospective employer.

You may be in the relatively fortunate position of having a clear idea of what your next career will be. In this case you should carry out the self-awareness exercises given below in order to check your decision, and explore whether this next career is likely to suit you. But many people who decide to leave teaching have only a hazy idea of what they want to do next—something along the lines of 'working for a charity' or 'going into computers', if not even vaguer. If you fit into this category then it is vital that you begin your career search by striving for a more definite notion of what your next career should be. After all, it is only when you know what you want that you can devote your energy to getting it!

## The self-awareness exercises

In this chapter there are many exercises which aim to increase your understanding of what aspects of work are important to you. However, you must be realistic about the limitations of these types of exercise. The Freuds and the Jungs of the world apart, self-analysis can go so far and no further. Even with enormous effort it is still extremely difficult (if not impossible) to be truly objective about ourselves. When confronted with a series of questions about what we are looking for in a job, our answers will reflect what we *think* we should be looking for, rather than what we actually want from a job.

We are all constrained by the expectations we have of ourselves, and the expectations that other people hold of us. Self-awareness is not a simple matter of working your way through a list of hundreds of exploratory questions as some careers books imply. Many American guides in particular seem to assume that if the list of questions is long enough you can gain the 'self-knowledge' that will form the basis of your direct ascent to a million-dollar career. If self-understanding was as easy as answering questions at the back of a book, all the counsellors, therapists, analysts (and couch makers) of the world would rapidly be out of business!

However, working through self-awareness exercises is *not* a waste of time. They can be illuminating as long as you are realistic about the depth of insight that they can provide. The exercises form a necessary starting-point for planning and carrying out your career change.

There are also better and worse ways of completing them. First, work through them on your own at a time when you have no distractions or interruptions. Second, give each answer the time that it deserves and continually ask yourself, 'is that really true?' and, 'do I actually think that?', in order to tease out what you really think from what you *think* you should think. Third, having completed the exercises, discuss your answers with different people. As an ideal, try three categories of confidante: a close friend/partner who knows you outside your work as a teacher; a teaching friend with whom you have worked, and lastly (and most difficult to find) someone you respect and trust but who is not a close personal friend. The two former categories of adviser have the advantage of knowing you very well but there is the danger that they will tell you what they think you want to hear. That's why people in the third category can be so useful.

## Thinking about teaching

Before you can work out what you want from your next career, you must start by doing some hard thinking about the time you spent as a teacher. Even the most disillusioned teacher enjoys a few aspects of the profession. Begin by working out what parts you find rewarding and what proves frustrating. This will give you a rough guide to the sort of work you should look for in the future.

### Exercise 1

1. Think back to the time when you decided to become a teacher. List all the factors that influenced this decision. Be honest with yourself. If one of the main factors was 'couldn't think what else to do with my degree' then say so. Clarifying your thoughts in this way could help prevent you from drifting into your second career.

2. Consider the factors listed above in Question 1.

   (a) Were any of them due to pressures that other people placed on you (eg entering teaching because your parents thought it was a suitable profession)?

   (b) If the answer to (a) is 'yes', how will you be able to control those external pressures in the future?

3. In what ways has teaching fulfilled your expectations for a satisfactory career?

4. Use your answer to Question 3 to list up to five characteristics that you want your next job to have.

5. In what ways has teaching as a career proved unsatisfactory?

6. Use your answer to Question 5 to list up to five characteristics that are absent in your present teaching post, but that you would want in your next job.

## What are you really like?

Remember the words of Oscar Wilde! 'To lose one parent... may be regarded as a misfortune; to lose both looks like carelessness.'

Prospective employers will understand why you want to change career once, but to embark on a major career change more than once may well look like 'carelessness'. You don't want to jeopardise your chances of finding a satisfactory career alternative by launching yourself into an entirely unsuitable career. The only way to avoid this is to have a good idea of your own personality.

Once you have decided what career you wish to pursue you will meet a number of people in the field, both in the fact-finding missions that you undertake (see Chapter 3) and also in interviews for vacant posts (see Chapter 5). Look at people who are successful in the area and ask yourself whether they have a similar outlook to yours. If you continually find yourself being interviewed by people whose personality and interests seem markedly different from your own, you are unlikely to be happy. All this presupposes that you have a clear idea of your personality.

*Exercise 2. How do you see yourself?*

1. Briefly make a list of 15-20 adjectives or phrases that best describe you.

*Exercise 3. How does someone else see you?*

1. Ask someone from each of the three categories of adviser to give a list of five to ten adjectives or phrases that they think best describe you.
2. With the adviser, compare the results of Exercises 2 and 3. In what ways does your self-perception overlap with that of someone else, and how does it differ? Discuss the differences and see whether an outsider's perception of you throws light on some interesting self-characteristics that you haven't considered.

*Exercise 4. How do people in authority see you?*
Describe yourself as seen through the eyes of someone who is superior to you at work, for example, your head of department. If you are a head of department/year yourself, then consider how you appear to the deputy head or head. (If possible follow up this exercise by asking the person concerned.)

1. In what ways does this person's view of you differ from your own self-perception?
2. Do these differences in perception lead to conflict? If so, how will this conflict be resolved in your next career?

*Exercise 5. What are your interests?*
There is one point on which all teachers would agree: pupils put the
most effort into those subjects that interest them, and into those
subjects where they are likely to do well. But this principle applies
beyond pupils. You will be happiest in a job where the work really
stimulates you, and you achieve good results. No one can be content if they are bored by their work, or where they feel that they are
not coping well with the tasks demanded of them. It is therefore
vital that you work out your interests.

Each of the questions will focus on things that interest you, and
which you enjoy doing. After each of the questions ask yourself
*why* you enjoy these activities. You should then start to see a pattern of interest emerging in the 'why' column.

1. List the five activities which you most enjoy.          Why?
2. When you read the daily or Sunday paper, which          Why?
   subjects do you choose to read?
3. If you had the chance to return to college and          Why?
   study anything, what would it be?
4. Think of a time in your life when you were most         Why?
   fulfilled. What were you doing?

**Identify your achievements and skills**

Imagine a typical school day morning. You arrive in school at 8.45
and have a brief discussion over a cup of coffee with the head of
year about a truanting pupil in your tutor group. Tutor period follows during which you talk to the truanting pupil, follow up a com-
plaint of misbehaviour from another member of staff, and collect
money from seven pupils for a school outing. Your first lesson is an
A-level class and you launch straight into an explanation of the
complexities of human genetics. After a 15-minute break the second period follows, which is a practical science lesson with a low
ability third-year group. At the outset you settle the class down
and carefully explain the purpose of the experiment. You then
organize the distribution of 25 pieces of apparatus and the class
carry out the practical work. Finally, you check the apparatus
back in, discuss the results of the experiment and set homework.

Period 3 is a 'free' period. A great misnomer if ever there was
one! You retreat to the staff office to phone the parents of your
truanting pupil. The parent complains that her child is being bull-
ied. After hearing the mother's point of view you stress that this
matter needs to be sorted out urgently, and you arrange a time for

the parents to come in and talk to the pastoral staff. You then walk back to your department intending to spend the remainder of your 'free' period planning lessons. A vexed probationary teacher comes into the departmental office saying that one pupil is disrupting the lesson and teaching the rest of the class is an impossibility.

The head of department has taken her class to the local park to carry out an ecological study and as no one else seems to be around to help out, you go back to the probationary teacher's class and tactfully extract the pupil, trying not to undermine the new teacher's authority. You settle the pupil down with some suitable task such as stapling worksheets in the departmental office and continue with your lesson planning until the bell goes. All this before lunch!

Most teachers would agree that this is a fairly typical school morning. But think of some of the different skills that you have had to put into practice: *counselling* pupils in your tutor group; *administering* the collection of money; teaching your subject to a *high academic level*; and *assisting* junior members of your department, to name but a few.

The important point is that you will not lose these skills once you step out of the classroom. Instead you must look upon them as assets which are readily transferable to your next career. If, for example, you decide to go into educational publishing, you can learn the specific details about the production and marketing of books on the job. At the interview the employer will be interested to find out if you have a clear idea as to what makes a good text book, if you can write clearly and can work well as part of a team. These are three skills that you will have developed as a teacher, and are transferring to the context of publishing.

The purpose of Exercises 6 and 7 is to focus on your achievements as a teacher, in order to identify the skills you built up in the course of your teaching career. One careers expert uses a constructive working definition of the word 'achievement': 'Something you yourself feel you have done well, that you have enjoyed doing and felt proud of.' Bear this definition in mind while completing these exercises.

*Exercise 6*

1. List 10-15 achievements of your teaching career. (You may also consider achievements in other spheres of your life, such as voluntary work or leisure activities.)

2. For each achievement, identify the skills involved. You need to push yourself at this point in order to uncover as many skills as possible.

3. Finally, describe how you and other people know the achievement was a success. This is important both for your own morale, and also for how you present yourself to other people. Intentions alone are insufficient. At an interview it is not enough to say that you spent a considerable amount of time trying to improve attendance in your tutor group. Instead you should tell the employer how you succeeded in having the lowest level of truancy in all the eight fifth-year classes in the school.

*Example:*

| *Achievement* | *Skills* |
|---|---|
| ● Developed a new active tutorial work programme for use with first-year tutor groups | ● Initiating, developing and seeing a project through to completion |
| | ● Identifying the pastoral needs of first-year pupils |
| | ● Working closely with other members of the pastoral team |
| | ● Analysing the suitability of available published material |
| | ● Writing/editing/designing our own material |

*How did I (or other people) know this achievement was a success?*

● Feedback from the consumer! Pupils stopped saying that tutor period was a waste of time

● Reduction in levels of bullying in first year

● Pastoral staff of neighbouring school asked if they could use our material

*Exercise 7*
You will need to enlist the help of your confidantes for this exercise. Read them the results of Exercise 6 and then ask them two further questions:

1. For any of the achievements, are there any obvious skills that you have omitted?

2. Can they see a pattern in terms of your achievements and skills?

By the time you have completed Exercises 6 and 7 your spirits should be lifting. The results of these exercises give you concrete evidence of all that you have achieved during your teaching career.

**Job qualities**

By this stage in the chapter you have already spent some time thinking about your personality and interests, and about what you achieved as a teacher. To be happy and fulfilled in your work there has to be a close fit between what you have to offer the job, given your personality, interests and skills, and the characteristics of the job itself. If you are a very sociable animal who loves working as part of a team, you will be miserable in a job that requires you to work in solitary confinement for most of the time. In addition to your own personality and interests (see previous exercises) you must also consider the sort of environment in which you want to work. This exercise aims to help you identify the qualities and characteristics of a job that are important to you.

*Exercise 8*

1. Consider each item listed below, and think about whether it is an important job characteristic for you. Must your next career have this characteristic if you are to be happy in the job, or is it unimportant to you?
2. For each item listed below, say why this characteristic is important/unimportant to you.

   (a) Status:            A job which is prestigious and has high status

   (b) Security:          A job where you are unlikely to be fired at short notice

   (c) Salary:            Earning more than you do as a teacher

   (d) Promotion:         Good opportunities for rapid or steady advancement

   (e) Independence:      Being expected to work on your own without constant supervision

   (f) Hours of work:     A job where flexible and/or long hours of work are demanded

   (g) Variety:           A job where the work itself changes

| (h) | Opportunities to learn: | A job where you constantly have to acquire new skills and expertise in order to carry out the work successfully |
|---|---|---|
| (i) | Intellectual challenge: | Work that stretches your mind |
| (j) | Helping and caring for others: | Using your skills to assist other people |
| (k) | Responsibility: | Being in charge of, and supervising the work of others |
| (l) | Creativity: | A job which requires you to innovate and use your imagination |
| (m) | Sociable work environment: | A job where there is opportunity to work closely with, and enjoy the company of colleagues |
| (n) | Ethical concerns: | A job where there is compatibility between your personal moral values and the nature of the work |
| (o) | Ease of journey: | A job which can be reached easily from your present home |
| (p) | Opportunity to travel: | A job where you will have to travel within the country or abroad |

**Working out the next step**

Now you need to pool the results of the self-analysis and begin identifying possible future careers for yourself. This next exercise enables you to summarise the insights that you have gained in working through this chapter.

*Exercise 9*
Read through the results of the previous exercises.

1. List five to ten skills that you want to be able to use in your next job, eg I want to use:
   (a) my ability to calm people down and defuse a potentially difficult situation
   (b) my ability to counsel people and help them to find their own solution to their problems

2. Describe five characteristics of a work environment in which you are most likely to be successful and fulfilled. Try to be as

specific as possible, eg I want to work in an environment where there is:

(a)  opportunity for me to travel

(b)  opportunity for me to supervise other people etc

3. Using your answers to Questions 1 and 2, list the different job areas that you are interested in and want to investigate further. You may arrive at a job with a definite title (eg social worker, computer programmer). Conversely, you may not know the exact job title, in which case just write down the general area and characteristics of the job, eg working as a researcher for a pressure group.

## The four stages

You can visualise the task of choosing your next career as having four stages:

Stage 1:  You do not have any idea about what you enjoy doing, nor what skills you possess.

Stage 2:  You know what you are good at and what you enjoy doing, but you have no idea what to do with your skills and talents.

Stage 3:  You know the general field in which you intend to employ your skills (advertising, publishing, working for a charity) but you haven't worked out your specific job within that field.

Stage 4:  You have decided upon both the field and the specific sort of job you want within that field.

By the time you have worked your way through the exercises in this chapter you should have proceeded beyond stages 1 and 2. But if you haven't, don't despair. Read through and think about your answers to the self-awareness exercises in order to build up a firm picture of what you want from a job. Then talk to as many people as possible from a wide variety of different fields and pick their brains. Tell them what you are looking for in a job and ask them for suggestions for possible careers you could pursue. Eventually your ideas will begin to clarify and you will know the direction in which you should be heading.

### Starting with the Encyclopedia

Teachers often set their younger pupils 'finding out' exercises for homework: find out about the *Cutty Sark*, Alexander Fleming, the widest river in the world, etc. Many children will head straight for the library encyclopedia when faced with a task of this kind. Now the tables are reversed, and it is time for you to consult the *Careers Encyclopedia* (1984), editor Audrey Segal, published by Cassell in association with the *Daily Telegraph*. It is available in many public libraries, and if your local branch library doesn't have a copy they will probably order one for you.

As soon as your ideas begin to clarify about the sort of job you want to pursue, the *Encyclopedia* will prove an invaluable resource. It provides a wealth of information, which can otherwise be obtained only by sifting your way through many different publications. It divides careers into a number of different broad areas (eg commerce/finance, central/local government, professional/scientific, and social services). A large number of careers within each area are discussed, with information about the nature of the work, promotion opportunities and qualifications needed. Each entry is quite brief, but suggestions for further reading and addresses of organisations which will provide additional information are also given.

If you feel that you haven't even decided what broad career area you want to pursue, the *Encyclopedia* can still be a great asset, as it enables you to look up the particular degree that you studied and find suggestions for a large range of careers that follow on well from your degree.

While you are carrying out this further reading, keep on referring back to the results of Exercise 9. Continually ask yourself whether the job you are reading about will meet the criteria you set out in that exercise.

### Signposts

*Signposts* (1983), published by the Careers and Occupational Information Centre (COIC), is another resource that you can consult if you need suggestions about possible careers to pursue. It is available in many public libraries.

*Signposts* consists of a series of reference cards, each one containing details about a particular career. Although it is designed for use with fifth and sixth formers, it provides an extremely useful job classification. There are two different indices. First, a subject classification. You can look up a particular subject (eg history) and find a list of jobs in which the subject has a *direct* bearing and a list of jobs in which the subject has *some* bearing. Second, there is a career type classification, eg scientific careers, general service careers etc. Within each 'career type' category many different suggestions are made. For each career included, the cards have information about job availability, training, aptitude and further addresses to contact.

## Equal Opportunities

*Equal Opportunities: A Careers Guide*, by Ruth Miller and Anna Alston, published by Penguin in 1984, also gives basic information about an enormous range of different careers. An important feature of this book is that each career summary includes details about the position of women and also how the profession views mature entrants. It is a particularly useful reference source for the career-changing teacher.

## Beyond self-analysis

The self-awareness exercises are useful as they get you thinking along the right lines. However, it may be impossible for you to reach a firm decision about alternative careers on the basis of the exercises and further reading alone. Luckily there are other resources which you can use in order to obtain further career guidance.

### 1. The Association of Graduate Careers Advisory Services (AGCAS)

The careers services of *every* university and polytechnic in the UK and Eire, plus a growing number of colleges of higher education, belong to an umbrella organisation called AGCAS. If you studied at a college of higher education (or at a now disbanded teacher-training college which has become a college of higher education), you can find out if your college belongs to AGCAS by contacting the AGCAS Central Services Unit (CSU) at:

Central Services Unit
Crawford House
Precinct Centre
Oxford Road
Manchester M13 9EP
*Tel:* 061-273 4233

A number of invaluable services are provided by the Central Services Unit of AGCAS.

## (a) Gradscope

Gradscope is a computer-aided exercise especially designed to help students in higher education and graduates to choose a suitable career. It consists of a questionnaire with 50 questions covering various aspects of work activities, working conditions and your own abilities and skills. Your answers are then fed into a computer containing the Gradscope program and you receive a print-out of suggested occupations which come closest to satisfying your stated priorities. The relative advantages and disadvantages of each occupation are compared in the light of your responses. In addition, appropriate career information sheets published by AGCAS, and other sources of reference, are suggested, so that you can consider the suggested occupations in greater depth.

There are a number of advantages to using Gradscope. As with the self-awareness exercises the process of answering the 50 questions can help you to become more aware of your own personal priorities. Furthermore, the 120 occupations in the Gradscope data bank are all open to graduates with any degree subject. Gradscope is therefore particularly useful if your degree is not vocationally oriented, or if you wish to explore possibilities other than those related to your own subject.

*Eligibility.* It does not matter how long ago you graduated for you to be eligible to use the Gradscope services. As the careers services of all polytechnics and universities in the country are affiliated to AGCAS, if you have a degree from *any* polytechnic or university you can use Gradscope. The really good news is that even if you obtained a teaching qualification from a teacher training college or college of higher education which is *not* affiliated to AGCAS, you can still use the Gradscope facility. To obtain the actual questionnaire, either contact the careers advisory service at your own polytechnic/university/college of higher education, or write direct to the Central Services Unit (CSU) at the address given on page 27.

Gradscope costs only £3, which covers the processing of the questionnaire, so it gives excellent value for money.

## (b) Career counselling interviews

The careers services of all universities and polytechnics in this country are usually willing to provide a graduation to grave service. This means that the careers service of your own university or polytechnic will probably see you for a career counselling interview, regardless of how many years ago you graduated. Bear in mind, though, that the relevance of the advice provided by the careers service is likely to decrease the further you get from your own graduation, as the services are aimed at helping current undergraduates and recent graduates.

Prior to 1977 the government-funded Occupational Guidance Units provided free career guidance for adults, but these units have now been disbanded. Nowadays obtaining career guidance or counselling is not so easy, and the high cost of the commercial agencies is discussed below. Therefore, if you feel that you need to consult a professional careers adviser your best bet is to begin by making contact with your polytechnic or university careers service.

Even though these careers services will see ex-students who graduated many years previously, their first priority is to help more recent students. Don't be put off if they don't offer you an interview within the next week or so: you may have to wait quite a while. It is better if you contact them during the college vacations or during their slightly less hectic period (the beginning of April until the end of September) as the college careers services tend to find that their work is heavily concentrated in the Christmas and Easter terms.

The more thought you give to your career plans *before* you see the careers adviser, the more you will get out of the interview and the more he will be able to help you. I would recommend that you carry out the self-awareness exercises given in this chapter and complete the Gradscope questionnaire before you have an interview with a careers adviser.

### (c) Mutual aid

AGCAS also operates a mutual aid scheme, so for example, if you are a graduate of Leicester Polytechnic working in Exeter, you are entitled to use some of the facilities of Exeter University careers service. Under the AGCAS mutual aid scheme, as a graduate of any UK/Eire polytechnic or university you are entitled to use the reference and library facilities of any polytechnic or university careers service. In practice, if you obtained your teaching qualification from a teacher training college or a college of higher education, no polytechnic or university careers service is likely to object to you using their library for reference, although this may not be strictly covered under the AGCAS mutual aid scheme. You do not need to make an appointment in advance in order to use the reference facilities.

Whether you are entitled to career counselling interviews under the mutual aid scheme differs from institution to institution. In the past such interviews were freely available under mutual aid.

One ex-teacher I interviewed, now a senior BBC journalist, had ten career counselling interviews at the careers service of her local polytechnic, despite the fact that she was a graduate of a different institution! Nowadays, although some careers advisory services are willing to offer perhaps one or two counselling interviews under mutual aid, others will only provide information facilities, and will insist that you return to your own higher education institution for career counselling.

In order to find out what mutual aid facilities are available at your local university or polytechnic careers service, you should consult a guide called *Graduate Careers Services* (1984), edited by Alex Nicholson and published by Newpoint Ltd (previously New Opportunity Press). This guide, available in many public reference libraries, lists all the university and polytechnic careers advisory services, and for most (but not all) entries, it discusses what mutual aid facilities are available. If you can't find a copy, or if the institution you are interested in is one of the vaguer entries, then ring up the careers advisory service and ask if they could offer you a career counselling interview under the mutual aid scheme. Make it clear that you are willing to come at any time that would be convenient for them, but don't be too disappointed if they tell you that career counselling is restricted to their own graduates.

Some careers advisory services (eg London University) have duty careers officers, and they will be able to give you very brief but immediate consultations. The service provided by the duty officer is *not* a full career counselling interview, but they may be able to answer a specific query, or tell you where you can find out further information. Once again, the duty officer will be able to give you more help if you come into the careers advisory service at an off-peak time, rather than at a time when there are 20 other people in the office all wanting answers to their questions.

### (d) AGCAS publications

AGCAS, through the operations of the Central Services Unit, produces a number of information booklets. Each booklet covers a particular occupation or occupational area. Included in each booklet are job descriptions (often first-hand accounts from people in the job, rather than the blander, more cosmetic descriptions put out by professional associations), details of qualifications needed, and suggestions for obtaining further information. The cost is £1.10 per booklet.

A particularly useful AGCAS booklet is 'Work related to education'. The following occupations are covered: educational administration; educational psychology; educational welfare work; counselling; youth work; careers advisory work; educational broadcasting; educational journalism; educational publishing; educational research; educational technology; education in industry; museum education; school libraries; health education; play projects; sports centres, field study centres and zoos!

If you have decided that you want to stay within education, but move out of the classroom, then begin by reading this booklet. To obtain this or any of the other booklets (or a free list of the 70 available titles) contact the Central Services Unit, at the address given on p.27.

## 2. Association of Careers Advisers in Colleges of Higher Education (ACACHE)

All the careers advisory services in colleges of higher education belong to this umbrella organisation. To complicate the matter further, 20 of these colleges of higher education also belong to AGCAS. If you studied at a college of higher education (or at a teacher training college which has now become a college of higher education) which is *not* affiliated to AGCAS, then you should get in contact with ACACHE at the address below:

ACACHE
Liverpool Institute of Higher Education
Woolton Road
Liverpool L16 8ND
*Tel:* 051-722 7331 (ext 292 or 295)
General Secretary: Raymond O'Connor

It was mentioned earlier that if you merely want to use a careers advisory service as a reference library, then it does not matter if you graduated from an institution that is not affiliated to AGCAS: your local university or polytechnic careers advisory service will not object to you using their reference facilities. However, even under the AGCAS mutual aid scheme career counselling interviews can be scarce, so if you graduated from an institution that is *not* affiliated to AGCAS, you have little hope of getting a career counselling interview in an AGCAS institution. But do not despair! ACACHE operates its own mutual aid scheme. All you need to do is get in touch with the organisation at the address given above. In turn, they will put you in contact with the careers advisory service of your local college of higher education, where you will be able to obtain career counselling.

### 3. National Advisory Centre on Careers for Women (NACCW)

The NACCW is an educational charity providing career advice and information for women. It provides career counselling to women of all ages so it can assist women wishing to change direction and also those wishing to return to a career after a break. Their only office is in London, so their career counselling service is only useful for people who live within travelling distance of London. The fee for a career counselling interview is £26.50 for a non-member of NACCW. Subsequent interviews cost £19. All fees are inclusive of VAT. In special circumstances charges may be reduced.

The NACCW can be contacted at:

Drayton House
30 Gordon Street
London WC1H 0AX
*Tel:* 01-380 0117

### 4. The Pepperell Unit of the Industrial Society

The Pepperell Unit is a unit within the Industrial Society, a registered educational charity which exists to promote a better understanding of the role of industry in society at large. One of its aims is to help women of all ages develop their skills, abilities and confidence, in order to allow them to make the most of their careers. The unit runs a number of courses that are relevant to the career-changing teacher. Some of the courses are only open to women, but many also welcome men, although they are likely to be in the minority. The 1986-7 calendar of events includes a number of one-day workshops run in conjunction with *Cosmopolitan* magazine. The following workshops are available: changing career direction; learning how to sell yourself; career development and setting up your own business. The cost of a place on one of these workshops is £35.00+VAT. It is worth noting that some of these events are also held outside London. A full list of courses can be obtained from:

The Pepperell Unit
The Industrial Society
Robert Hyde House
48 Bryanston Square
London W1H 7LN
*Tel:* 01-262 2401

## 5. Lifeskills Associates

Barrie Hopson and Mike Scally were formerly director and deputy director of the Counselling and Career Development Unit at Leeds University. In 1984 they left the university and founded an organisation called Lifeskills Associates. This organisation produces a wide range of excellent resources and also provides career counselling interviews and workshops. Their address is:

Lifeskills Associates
Clarendon Chambers
51 Clarendon Road
Leeds LS2 9NZ
*Tel:* 0532 467128

The following publications and facilities which they provide are particularly relevant to the career-changing teacher.

### (a) Build Your Own Rainbow

A workbook for career and life management, by Barrie Hopson and Mike Scally (price £10.25 including postage and packing). This workbook goes far beyond the self-awareness exercises given in this chapter. It is a comprehensive approach to career planning including not only exercises about working out your interests, transferable skills, etc, but also giving information and exercises on topics such as stress management and the psychology of different adult life stages.

*Build Your Own Rainbow* consists of 40 varied exercises aiming to help you answer questions such as 'How satisfied am I?', 'What changes do I want?' and, 'How do I make them happen?'. In the process of answering these questions the workbook helps you to develop fundamental career (and life) management skills, for example, research skills, decision-making and the ability to learn from your experiences. It is well written and produced and is much the best book of its kind available. Copies can be bought directly from Lifeskills Associates.

### (b) Work Choices—an Open University community education short course

This short course uses *Build Your Own Rainbow* as its study book, and it forms the basis of the course. In addition, if you decide to work through the *Build Your Own Rainbow* workbook by taking the OU short course, you will also be provided with:

- A course guide helping you to organise your approach to the course.
- Two audio-cassettes providing illustrative case studies of people working through the exercises in the workbook and talking about their own career and life changes
- Specially prepared booklets on self-employment, job finding, interview skills and surviving unemployment
- Regular and individualised computer-generated reports, in response to questions you complete as part of the course.

*Work Choices* costs £29.95 (including package and posting). Full details can be obtained from:

> LMSO
> The Open University
> PO Box 188
> Milton Keynes MK3 6HW

### (c)  Individual career counselling

This service is less expensive than most of the commercial agencies because clients use a specially designed computer program called *Career Builder* which reduces the time the client needs to spend with the counsellor.

*Career Builder* is a much more extensive enterprise than Gradscope, although it is also more expensive. With *Career Builder* you identify your work values, occupational interests, transferable skills and preferred career pattern. The program builds on this information and enables you to set objectives and plan your next career step. You are also given methods of discovering what kinds of work, education and training match your skills.

The cost of two hours using *Career Builder*, plus a 15-minute brief counselling interview, is £30. Additional counselling costs £25 per hour, but many people find after using the *Career Builder* program that they don't need any further help, and for most people one hour of career counselling is sufficient. The snag is that this service is only available at the Lifeskills Associates office in Leeds.

### (d)  Career development workshops

Lifeskills Associates provide career development workshops for people in a wide range of different settings. These workshops aim to help people examine their careers, set appropriate career objectives and develop action plans to implement them. A variety of training methods is used including individual, pairs and small group work. Some pre-course work is usually set.

The organisation has considerable experience of working with teachers, and it runs workshops for teachers who are considering changing their careers. If you get together with colleagues and form a group of ten teachers, Lifeskills Associates will arrange a weekend workshop for you in Leeds, at a cost of £60 per person, excluding food and accommodation.

## 6. Career and Educational Counselling

Career and Educational Counselling is a unit of the Tavistock Centre in London. It consists of a group of psychologists who provide a career counselling service. The approach used is very different from that of the traditional vocational guidance agencies; the aim is not to tell you what you should be doing, or even what you are good at doing. Instead, using a psychotherapeutic perspective, the counsellor will help you to explore internal as well as external reasons why you may be experiencing dissatisfaction with your work. In this way, any decisions you make about your future will be based on an increased understanding of yourself and your needs.

If you want to find out factual careers information ('Is computer programming an expanding field/Will I be accepted for training with a third class degree?' etc) then this type of career counselling is not appropriate. But if you feel that you could benefit from exploring what work means to you, and why you are currently feeling unfulfilled, then Career and Educational Counselling may provide the approach you need.

Clients usually have between two and five interviews, although some have more. The initial session (1½ hours) costs £30+VAT, but subsequent sessions (1 hour) cost £17+VAT. A reduced fee can be arranged for the unemployed.

The address is:

Career and Education Counselling
The Tavistock Centre
120 Belsize Lane
London NW3 5BA
*Tel:* 01-794 1309 (answerphone)

## 7. Private vocational guidance agencies

The services provided by the private vocational guidance agencies, though more extensive than those offered by the polytechnic/

university careers advisory services, are also expensive. The agencies differ among themselves in the services they provide and the fees they charge, but there are broad similarities between them.

The consultation is likely to last a day. Before visiting the consultants you will probably be sent a detailed personal history form to fill in which will provide a background to the interview. On the morning of the consultation you will carry out a number of psychometric tests measuring characteristics such as aptitude, interests, personality and attainment. A career consultation will follow in the afternoon in which you review the test results and discuss career possibilities. Finally, you will be sent a written report giving you details of the test results, and a summary of the discussion you had with the consultant, including the suggestions made during the interview. Further addresses and other sources of information to enable you to apply for the courses and careers recommended will be included. The fee for this service is likely to be in the range of £150-£200+VAT.

London University careers advisory service has produced some excellent guidance notes for their students who are considering using private agencies. They point out that the private agencies tend to place a greater reliance on psychometric tests than on the counselling type interviews provided by the polytechnic/university careers advisory services. As a result the private agencies often take a more prescriptive role, advising you what you *should* do, rather than working from a counselling viewpoint where the emphasis is on helping you to make your own decisions.

Furthermore, the agencies probably have much less information about courses, job openings, and the 'state-of-the-market' than the careers advisory services. In the past the private agencies have been criticised for advising people to pursue opportunities in certain fields, when in reality the openings in that area were almost non-existent.

Finally, the London University careers advisory service leaflet stresses:

> Before you commit yourself to anything with a private agency, be absolutely certain that you get *in writing* a statement of the fees that will be incurred.

Take heed of this advice!

In summary, if all the other options mentioned above have failed and you haven't a clue what career direction you should be pursuing then consider using a private vocational guidance agency. They have helped put some people on the right path. But think about it very seriously before you commit yourself to spending large sums of money.

The addresses of vocational guidance agencies can be obtained from the Education Guardian in Tuesday's *Guardian*.

## Help for the unemployed teacher

If you are an unemployed teacher who is looking for jobs *outside* the teaching profession, many of the suggestions already discussed in this chapter may be relevant to you. In addition, Bridge Programme courses may be of particular interest. These part-time Manpower Services Commission (MSC) courses are aimed at helping unemployed professional people get back to work. If you don't know what career you want to pursue, you are first provided with extensive career guidance. Having chosen your career, the course covers ways of improving your chances of getting a job by giving you practice interviews, and helping you with CV preparation and job applications. At the Polytechnic of Central London Bridge Programme there is a success rate of 75 per cent.

For further details, contact the MSC Training Division Office in your area.

*Chapter 3*

# How to Find Out More About Your Next Career

Choosing your next career will be one of the major decisions of your life—perhaps not quite as monumental as deciding to get married or to start a family, but certainly an extremely important step. In order to ensure that you move in the right direction, you must find out as much as possible about your new career before you take any irretrievable steps. This involves two strategies. First, read as much as possible about the work and second, talk to people who do the job you are interested in. Don't regard these as Step One and Step Two as you will continually be going back and forwards between the two. The people you meet will direct you towards new things to read, and in the light of this reading you may want to get answers to more questions.

You might think that reading alone is sufficient, and you can get by without going to talk to people in the field, but this can be a grave mistake. For example, imagine that you have decided you want to become an educational psychologist. Perhaps the prospect of helping children with learning difficulties or the opportunity to work with children and their families appeals to you.

You have written to the relevant professional association (in this case the British Psychological Society) for information about the nature of the work, salary, prospects and training. After reading through this information, the picture of an educational psychologist's work still sounds attractive. Next you get in contact with a practising educational psychologist and ask him or her about the work. A different picture starts to emerge. From the psychologist you find out that the work involves considerable use of psychological tests. Moreover, you discover that, like the GP, the role of the psychologist is to diagnose learning difficulties and make recommendations, rather than actually embarking on any remedial teaching or counselling.

This type of work may fascinate the educational psychologist that you talk to, but you know from working through the previous chapter that you want to be able to develop a relationship with your pupils over a period of time, rather than having a one-off diagnostic role. If you hadn't gone and talked to a practising educational psychologist you might have launched yourself into a new career which would prove to be no nearer to the career you want than your current teaching job. It is vital that you supplement the written information obtained from careers guides, and the information sent out by professional organisations, with a face-to-face talk with someone who actually does the job.

## Where to find out about different careers

Preliminary reading about different careers was given in the previous chapter (pp.26-7). You should have begun your reading by looking up the career in Cassell's *Careers Encyclopedia* and then gone on to see if one of the 70 titles produced by AGCAS covers your career of interest. In addition, your local university or polytechnic careers service can provide information about a wide range of careers.

A further basic reference source to consult is *Occupations*, published by COIC. This is a comprehensive annual publication available in good public reference libraries, containing details of 280 different careers. Each career article contains the following details: the work; work environment; pay and conditions; opportunities and prospects; personality types suited to the work; entry requirements; training, and related occupations.

For many careers there will be a professional or trade association that is worth consulting. You will get the name and address of the relevant association from a general careers guide such as the *Careers Encyclopedia* or *Occupations*. An alternative way of finding out the name of the association (which may be necessary if you intend to pursue a somewhat esoteric career) is to consult the *Directory of British Associations*, published by CBD Research Publications. This excellent directory—as its name suggests—lists all the associations in the UK. In addition, it also gives basic information about the activities of the association, eg whether they publish a newsletter or a journal.

Having worked out which association to consult, write them a short letter and ask for information about how you enter the profession, whether further training is necessary, prospects (ie are numbers of people in the profession increasing or decreasing) attitude towards mature entrants, and salary. You should also ask for details about any journals, magazines or newsletters published by the association. Reading through a professional or trade publication can give you considerable background information, which will also prove particularly useful in interviews. However, before you send off the subscription for a journal, see if you can obtain a copy from the library. Some professional journals are extremely expensive and very dull.

## Talk to someone in the field

It is vital that you go and talk to someone who is currently working in your field of interest. In fact, you should aim to talk to more than one person, to avoid being unduly influenced by one person's view of their job, when it might be idiosyncratic and unrepresentative of the field as a whole.

The problem is how to find these people. You may be lucky enough to know someone who does the job or, second best, know someone who in turn knows someone else. In terms of finding suitable contacts, as with so many other aspects of changing career, it is important to 'pick the brains' of all your friends and relatives.

I am not suggesting that you advertise the fact that you are intending to change career to the whole staffroom. A career change can be a slow process, and you don't want staffroom bores making jokes at your expense, when you haven't yet made a successful move. But do talk widely among your close friends and family. Once you have decided on your next career, ask them if they know anyone who is a landscape gardener, graphic designer, speech therapist etc. You may well be successful in finding a suitable contact this way.

A drama teacher, now a drama therapist working in a psychiatric hospital, had this to say:

> I kept on harassing friends, and friends of friends who were in the field I was interested in. It was very useful as each contact led to another person, book, course or job to investigate. If you are nice to contacts, they don't mind giving up their time to see you.

It would be unrealistic to claim that asking your friends and family will produce contacts in all possible jobs. Not everyone has a family as large as Peter Rabbit, or perhaps you are looking for a contact in a somewhat unusual job. If asking your friends and family fails to get you a lead into your career of interest, then you will need to adopt a different tactic. Ask yourself where people doing this work are found. With some jobs, there will be a straightforward answer to this question. For example if you want to work in hospital administration, then write to the relevant department at your local hospital. Addressing the letter to the 'senior administrator' at the hospital would probably yield a reply in the end, but it is better if you can sort out the name and specific job title of the person and address it personally to him or her. This can be done by phoning the hospital and asking to be put through to the administration department. Once you have reached the correct department ask the secretary for the name and job title of the head of department. You then know exactly to whom the letter should be addressed.

The *Yellow Pages* is another useful reference source. Look up the job in question, and unless you are interested in a very obscure career you may well find a list of people who work in the field. Once again, you can just direct your letter to 'Dear Sir or Madam' and send it off to the address given in *Yellow Pages*. However, it is better if you ring the organisation first, and ask for the name and job title of a relevant person in the organisation. Try to avoid getting involved in a long discussion with the secretary as to why you want this person's name, as the secretary may then tell you that their boss is far too busy to answer enquiries of your kind. But if the secretary is persistent, say that you have phoned up the organisation as they are your local solicitors/large department store/ community centre and that you wish to talk to someone who works in the field about current opportunities and prospects. Stress that you are not asking them for a job, merely for information, and you will not take up much of their boss's time. In this way you will usually succeed in getting the person's name and job title.

If the *Yellow Pages* doesn't yield the desired result, you still don't need to despair. Go back to the relevant trade or professional association, using the *Directory of British Associations*. Write to them or phone them, saying that you want to talk to a member of the profession in order to find out more about the nature of their work, and could they give you the names and addresses of association members working in your area.

### Writing the letter to your contact

A letter to an unknown person in your career of interest needs to be brief and to the point. If the letter is to yield results it must also be neatly handwritten or typed on good quality A4 paper, and be free of spelling mistakes or visible corrections. As with the preliminary telephone call to the organisation, it is also vital that you make two points clear: you are not asking for a job and you only expect a brief meeting.

A sample introductory letter is given on page 42.

You may find that you need to push yourself in order to write and

Mrs C Hampton MIPM
Senior Personnel Manager
Jones and Daughter plc
York YO1 2AA

2 June 1986

Dear Mrs Hampton

I would like to leave the teaching profession to re-train in the field of personnel management. I have written to the Institute of Personnel Management and read their literature as well as a number of books that they suggested.

I would very much like the opportunity to talk to an experienced personnel manager. I am not asking you to see me in the secret hope that you will be able to offer me a job! Instead, my aim is to talk to a senior member of the profession about the nature of personnel work itself.

As the field of personnel management is highly competitive, changing careers will be very hard. It is therefore all the more important that I talk to someone in the field, before I apply for a place on a suitable training course. I realize that you are extremely busy, but I would be very grateful if you could spare half an hour of your time to see me.

Yours sincerely

send off a letter of this kind. However, most people receiving a letter like this will either agree to see you, or give you the name of someone else who will. It is, after all, quite flattering to be thought of as an experienced person in one's field.

## Meeting the contact

On the face of it, the prospect of meeting your contact probably seems as daunting as having an interview. But remember, it isn't like an interview as you are not expecting your contact to offer you a job. The purpose of the meeting is for you to find out about the career in question, so don't cast yourself in the role of nervous interviewee who has to outshine the other (non-existent) candidates.

Bearing in mind the purpose of the meeting, it is clear that you must go well prepared. Make sure (as claimed in your letter to the contact) that you have done your background reading about the field. Paradoxically, the more initial reading you have done, the more useful the meeting is likely to be. For example, you may have found out from your reading that personnel work involves different tasks such as responsibility for recruitment and negotiating with employees' representatives. Perhaps the former task interests you, while the latter does not. In this situation it is sensible to ask whether the latter tends to be a large part of a personnel manager's work.

One point that you must explore with your contact is whether the field is expanding or contracting. If it emerges during the discussion that opportunities in the field are static or on the decline, you will need to think very seriously before pursuing opportunities in the field.

It is impossible to give a complete list of questions that you should pose to your contact, but the list below contains some useful suggestions.

- What do you actually do in an average day/week?
- What aspects of your work do you particularly enjoy?
- Are there any aspects of your work that you find frustrating?
- Would I need to embark on re-training to succeed in this job? If so, where are the best places to do the course?
- What is the attitude towards mature entrants in this field?
- Where are places on training courses/job vacancies advertised?
- What are the promotion prospects in this career?
- Would you advise someone to go into this field?
- Will the job give me mobility, or will I find it difficult to get work outside the major cities?
- Do you think my background in teaching is relevant in any way to this work?

Throughout this discussion you need to keep the results of the previous chapter in mind. Think back to the list of skills that you want to be able to use in your new job, and to your description of the work environment in which you hope to work. As you build up a clearer picture of what your contact actually does in his or her daily work, keep on asking yourself whether this matches your requirements in terms of your skills and ideal work environment.

Perhaps you will begin to entertain doubts, for example, if you think that the work is too solitary, and you would be happier in an environment where there is greater opportunity for teamwork. If this happens, ask your contact about this aspect of the work, and find out whether it is a necessary feature of the job, or whether it varies between different organisations. Try not to leave the interview with doubts that you haven't explored, as it may be difficult to go back and trouble this particular contact on a second occasion.

### After the meeting

Make sure that you have some time by yourself after the meeting to reflect on the discussion. Think about whether the career you had in mind still appeals to you and whether you want to continue pursuing jobs in this direction. Then, make a list of suggested reading or further contacts to write to that emerged from the interview, and follow these up as soon as possible.

Finally, before the day is out you must write a brief letter to your contact. In the letter thank them for giving up their time to see you and say that the opportunity to talk to someone in the field has helped you to clarify your ideas (even if it hasn't!). If you felt that you built up a good rapport you may also want to add that you will keep them informed about your career progress. But if you say this, you must be as good as your word—and remember to write to them when your career plans begin to crystallise. As a matter of courtesy, if a contact gives you particularly helpful advice which results in your finding a place on a suitable training course or getting a job, it is a nice idea to write and tell them about your success.

If you feel that your first contact wasn't particularly helpful and left many questions unanswered, repeat the whole process, and go and find a second contact. Perhaps the first person was relatively inexperienced themselves and didn't have a broad knowledge of the field. However, obtaining good on-the-job information is so essential that you must persevere until you have talked to (preferably) two good contacts.

### Voluntary opportunities

If you are interested in certain fields, for example social work or counselling, there is ample opportunity for you to carry out relevant voluntary work. Doing some voluntary work has two advantages: first, it allows you to find out much more about the nature of the work than can be learnt from reading books or talking to people in the field, and second, relevant voluntary experience will increase your chances of getting on a suitable training course or obtaining a job. Obviously teaching full-time is extremely demanding, and you may not have much time left over, but an evening a week or a fortnight, or voluntary work in the holidays, can provide invaluable experience.

It is important that the voluntary work matches your career interests as closely as possible. If, for example, you are thinking about becoming a school counsellor, then try to get voluntary work in a youth advisory centre, rather than in the local old people's home. Begin by asking your contact if suitable voluntary work exists, and if so, how you should go about obtaining it. The back page of *New Society* magazine has a weekly noticeboard listing a large number of different voluntary projects that require help. Furthermore, you can contact your local Volunteer Bureau (the Citizens Advice Bureau or public library will have the address and telephone number) to find out what voluntary opportunities are available in your area.

Although most voluntary opportunities are linked to the 'helping professions', commercial organisations may also take you on in a voluntary capacity. While still teaching, the trainee architect in my sample contacted a local architect's office who agreed to employ her as a volunteer during school holidays. Then, after the second voluntary period the architect started paying her a small salary. Through this work she gained practical experience and was able to demonstrate the extent of her commitment—two factors which helped her to be accepted on to a suitable training course.

## Where to find job vacancies

Some authors, in particular Richard Nelson Bolles in his American bestseller *What Colour is Your Parachute?*, strongly argue that the way to a good job does not lie in replying to job adverts. Bolles firmly states his position:

> The average job-hunter is almost sure that the job-hunting task consists—in one way or another—of unearthing jobs which someone held before, and which are now vacant. So the job-hunter searches classified ads, employment agencies etc. It rarely occurs to them that if, instead, you select the organisations or companies that interest you, and do enough research to unearth their problems (and how you can help solve them), the company may be perfectly willing to create a new job, for which no vacancy exists.

If between 60 and 70 per cent of jobs are filled by means *other than* job adverts, then one has to give serious consideration to Bolles' argument. Concentrating exclusively on the advertised job market may well have its limitations. However, there are also a number of important provisos to consider. America is very different from Britain and the approach which Bolles suggests is rather better suited to the other side of the Atlantic. Whereas many American organisations would see a person who has thoroughly researched a problem and approaches the organisation with its solution as an innovative answer to their prayers, in England that same person might be perceived as a pushy upstart.

Furthermore, even in England Bolles' strategy is more applicable to certain career areas than to others. For example, opportunities in local government or the Health Service cannot be created, but depend on a rigid allocation of funds. No matter how bright you are, or how perceptive your insight into the problems of a hospital administration department, the head of department will not be able to create a job for you out of nowhere. Conversely, in the private sector, particularly in its more innovative areas such as advertising, Bolles' approach might pay off. It is worth asking your contact how they think this type of approach might be regarded.

You must realise that Bolles' strategy is far from a doddle, and requires considerably more effort and initiative than replying to job adverts or going through agencies. Bolles clearly points out that the success of his strategy rests on the most careful and painstaking research and preparation. All the steps in this process are clearly outlined in his book. If this method appeals to you, and if your contact thinks that it might be successful, then the best advice is to refer you back to the English edition of *What Colour is Your Parachute?*, published in 1983 by Ten Speed Press.

### Newspapers and journals

Job advertisements are carried in a vast number of different publications ranging from the national dailies and Sunday papers to local newspapers and specialist trade and professional journals. In order to find out which publication carries adverts for vacancies in your field of interest, you need to do two things. First, ask your contact in the field or write to the relevant trade/professional association and ask them where vacancies are advertised. Second, in your reference library look at a guide called *Finding Job Vacancies*, which is a Careers Research and Advisory Centre (CRAC) publication. This guide provides the following information about different careers:

1. Where to find job adverts—which journals and newspapers carry vacancies
2. Placement agencies
3. Addresses of relevant organisations to consult

4. Lists of directories and other sources of information

5. A cross-reference to related jobs.

**Other publications to consult**

*Executive Post* is a weekly publication produced by PER—Professional and Executive Recruitment. PER is a section within the government-funded MSC, and provides a recruitment service for those seeking professional, scientific, technical and managerial employment. If you possess a teaching certificate or a degree then you are eligible to enrol with PER and you can enrol whether you are working or unemployed. Once you have enrolled, a free copy of *Executive Post* will be sent to you each week, for a maximum period of two years. The paper carries adverts for hundreds of jobs in a wide range of professional and executive areas. In addition to the job adverts, the paper also carries information about self-employment and places on MSC-funded training schemes. Enrolment forms for PER can be obtained from your local Jobcentre.

However, bear in mind that although PER is the largest professional recruitment agency in the country, it only carries adverts for those jobs which employers have asked (and paid) PER to fill. So the actual usefulness of *Executive Post* depends upon whether the sort of job you are interested in is often handled by PER. But as you can receive *Executive Post* for free, it is certainly worth your while to look through it each week, to see if it contains any interesting vacancies.

*Current Vacancies* is produced by the Central Services Unit of AGCAS and is available fortnightly throughout the year. It contains details of immediate vacancies for graduates of all disciplines, with or without experience. This publication can be mailed first class to you on the day of publication at a cost of £3.00 for six issues. An application form for *Current Vacancies* can be obtained from:

Central Services Unit
Crawford House
Precinct Centre
Oxford Road
Manchester M13 9EP
*Tel:* 061-273 4233

Alternatively, all university or polytechnic careers advisory services, and some colleges of higher education careers advisory services and public libraries, will have copies of *Current Vacancies* that you can consult. It is advisable to look at a copy of the publication in a library or careers advisory service to see if it contains relevant job vacancies, before you commit yourself to a subscription.

*Details of employers taking on graduate trainees*
*The Essential Guide to Graduate Opportunities*, published by New Opportunity Press (now Newpoint), is *not* a list of current vacancies, but it is an annual guide to the leading organisations that take on graduate trainees in all fields. It gives comprehensive information on the types of graduate they are looking for, the training, salary, benefits and times to apply. Using the index if you know the sort of work you are interested in, you can look up the organisations that recruit graduates in the field and write directly to them.

In addition, there are two other directories that you should consult: *Graduate Employment and Training*, published annually by CRAC, and *Directory of Opportunities for Graduates* (4 volumes), published annually by New Opportunity Press (now Newpoint).

To some extent these three directories overlap, but each one includes organisations not listed in the other two. To ensure that you are exploring all possibilities, you should consult all three.

*Chapter 4*

# CVs, Letters and Application Forms

Having worked through the skills exercises in Chapter 2, and carried out research into your chosen field as detailed in Chapter 3, you should have a good idea of the sort of job that interests you. This chapter is concerned with the stages involved in applying for a job, from deciding which job advertisements you should follow up, to constructing a first-rate CV and application form.

## Deciding whether to apply for the post

When you see an advertisement for a job that appeals to you, begin by asking yourself two questions. First, 'Do I want the job?', and second, 'Given my background in teaching, have I any chance of getting it?'. To consider the first question, the skills exercises of Chapter 2 will have enabled you to build up a picture of the sort of job that you want. From the job description in the paper, and from any further details that the employer has sent, you will be able to tell if the job meets your criteria. You will also need to consider this question from a practical point of view: will the salary be so low that you won't be able to keep up with the mortgage, and is the job within reasonable travelling distance?

Moving on to question two, it hardly needs saying that there are lots of jobs that we would dearly love, but that are never going to come our way. You may have decided after a successful career as an English teacher that you want to try to break into the highly competitive field of educational broadcasting. Don't waste your time applying for the post of Head of Educational Broadcasting at the BBC, however much the job would appeal to you! To answer this second question seriously, you need to distinguish between the mandatory and the secondary qualifications and experiences stated in the job advertisement. For example, a recent advertisement for the post of Press Officer with a national medical organisation is given below:

> Applicants must be non-smokers with at least three years' experience as a Press Officer. Experience of work in a health-related area would be useful.

If your only suitability for the mandatory part of the job description tion is that you are a non-smoker, ie you don't have three years' experience as a press officer, then don't waste your time applying for the job. Even if you have had considerable experience of working in a health-related field, for example organising the health education curriculum of your school, you will still not be considered for the post.

Employers are likely to be more flexible about the secondary aspects of the post. An advertisement for a research worker on a project studying the difficulties of adults returning to tertiary education stated:

> The post-holder must be a graduate with experience of carrying out research. Familiarity with the FE system would be helpful.

If you are a graduate with research experience (more than an undergraduate research project would be assumed), then it would be worth applying for this post, even if you have no familiarity with the FE system. Moreover, as a teacher you should point out in your application that you have direct experience of the secondary system, and indirect experience of FE through old students, and through colleagues who may have gone on to teach in the tertiary sector.

The guiding principle is that applying for a job is an all-or-nothing affair. If you think that there is some chance that you could get the post, even if you judge that this chance is extremely slight, you should put all your effort into the application. Conversely, if you feel that you haven't got the slightest chance of getting the post, don't waste any time applying for it. What you mustn't say to yourself is that even though you know you haven't got a chance, you'll just dash off a quick form anyway.

However, life is not as clear-cut as this advice suggests, and one is often confronted with grey areas. What should you do if you see an advert for a post that really interests you, but you think your chances of being successful are in the highly-unlikely-to-downright-impossible part of the spectrum? In this situation, you don't want to waste a lot of time filling in a form that will get you nowhere, but equally you don't want to miss possible job openings. The answer is to telephone the personnel manager, or whoever is mentioned in the advert, and ask if they will consider someone with your background.

When you have been put through to the personnel department, begin by asking if it is a convenient time to talk, or whether the personnel manager would prefer you to call back later. This shows that you are aware that the person on the other end of the telephone may be working under great pressure, and it also gives a courteous impression. If it is an inconvenient time the personnel manager will probably say so, which gives you the opportunity of telephoning back later when your call will be received more favourably.

You must prepare for the telephone call adequately. Have your question written down on a piece of paper in case your nerve fails, and also jot down all your experiences and skills that you feel would be relevant to the post. The worst that can happen is the employer tells you not to bother to apply, and at least you haven't wasted your valuable time. Alternatively, the employer may like the sound of your voice, and be impressed by the initiative you have shown, and tell you that they look forward to receiving your application.

Using this tactic, the trainee architect in my sample fixed herself up with holiday work in an architect's office. She rang up a firm that had an advertised vacancy and asked if they would consider someone with her background. The firm said 'No', but agreed after further discussion to take her on as an unpaid volunteer, and later this developed into paid work.

The greyest of all grey areas is likely to be age. Each year, there are numerous opportunities for fresh graduates to enter industry as part of a particular company's graduate traineeship scheme. But when does a recent graduate stop being recent? I contacted the personnel managers of a large number of companies who were advertising for graduate trainees. The consensus was that a graduate who was under 30 could still be considered for a trainee post, although the specific cut-off point will vary from company to company. So, if you are under 30, have decided that you want to go into industry, and you have a degree in the required subject, ring up and ask the personnel department whether they will consider you.

A number of personnel managers pointed out that the covering letter accompanying the CV would be all-important. As an experienced teacher rather than a recent graduate, you are a bit out of the ordinary. If you send in your CV and a letter which doesn't adequately explain your position you will probably be consigned to the rejection pile. Instead you must point out in your letter that not only do you possess a degree in the required subject but also your understanding of the academic content of your degree has been greatly increased through the experience of teaching the subject, and furthermore you have experience of the world of work, rather than coming straight from college or university.

What about applying for jobs where the advert states that no specific skills or experience are required? Two examples are given below:

A major London media department requires graduates to train as TV air time buyers. The successful applicant will be personable, numerate and ambitious!

Local theatre requires a house manager. Previous experience is not essential. Enthusiasm and interest in the theatre are more important.

You might think that you have a greater chance of being successful with these kinds of post. Although it is true that you won't be ruled out from the start because of your lack of previous relevant experience, you must realise that the number of applicants for these jobs will be all the greater, and therefore your chances are actually quite slim. You need to get the pessimism/optimism balance right: don't set your heart on any of these posts, but equally, try to remember that *somebody* has to get the job, so it is probably worth applying for them.

## Two words of warning

If you want to pursue a career in a very competitive area such as publishing, journalism or television, and you possess basic secretarial skills, you may be tempted to apply for secretarial posts in these fields. Bear in mind, however, that if you are currently on anything other than a Scale 1 salary, the salary offered for the secretarial post will be significantly lower, which will make the employer suspicious about offering you an interview, let alone a job. Particularly in large organisations, the division between secretarial and non-secretarial posts is frequently uncrossable. Prospects for promotion from the typewriter are likely to be slightly better in smaller companies. Moreover, if you are a bright ex-teacher who is interviewed for a secretarial post, you may well find that the personnel department do not take kindly to your questions about the likelihood of being promoted to more stimulating work. After all, the company is trying to get someone to type letters and answer the phone, and if they think you are over-qualified and ambitious, they will simply appoint a safer, less talented candidate.

The second word of caution concerns careers in selling. The classified pages contain a large number of adverts for posts in this area. Teaching involves 'selling' your subject to the pupils, so it is rightly seen to provide a good grounding in salesmanship. In fact, the back pages of the TES always have advertisements for teachers who want to branch out into this area. Undoubtedly some of these posts are genuine, but some pay appallingly low basic salaries, and the rest of the generous-sounding salary will actually depend on the commission. If the job involves trying to sell a less than first-rate product to people who don't want to buy it anyway, it will probably prove very frustrating, and you are unlikely to earn much of the commission component of the salary. You must check the salary structure—how much is basic, and how much rests on commission—before you spend any time in applying for the post.

## Having found a job to apply for—what next?

Always begin by being systematic in your job-search campaign. Cut out the job advert from the paper (or photocopy it if it is a library copy), and write down the name of the publication and the date of the issue.

Just like taking an exam, where it is essential to read the question, you must read the job advert carefully, and do *exactly* what the advert specifies. As in applying for teaching posts, one of two different routes is likely to be mentioned. Either you will be asked to send your CV and a letter of application, or you will be told to write off for an application form. In the latter case, don't waste your time sending a long explanatory covering letter and a CV, simply write a brief letter asking for the application form and any further relevant details to be sent to you.

## How to write first-rate CVs and application forms

Writing CVs and application forms that will do you justice takes time. You need to start by collecting all the necessary information about yourself into a 'personal data bank'. The categories of information which you should consider are given in the sample personal data bank on pp.60-66. These categories should not be regarded as immutable; you may decide that some are irrelevant or that there are others which you would like to include. However, the categories provide a starting point.

Constructing a personal data bank has a number of advantages:

● You will be able to construct CVs and application forms which best display your suitability, as you won't forget to mention anything relevant that you have done in the past.

● The information you collect in the personal data bank forms the basis of your covering letter or the 'why should we give this job to you' section of application forms.

- Systematically collecting information in this way speeds writing the mundane factual parts of CVs and application forms. You won't need to go rummaging through old address books and diaries to find out scraps of information such as the correct address and telephone number of one of your previous jobs.

- Assembling this information is an excellent preparation for interviews, helping you to analyse critically all that you have done in the past.

## The CV

CV is an abbreviation for curriculum vitae, ie the course of your life. You should think of your CV as an outline of the skills and experience that you can offer the employer, and you must structure it in terms of the requirements of the job. It may be necessary for you to do a fresh CV for each of your job applications. Certainly if you are applying for a variety of different types of job, then each job type will need a different CV. The task of constructing specific CVs for specific jobs isn't quite as daunting as it sounds; all you have to do is to augment the sections of your CV which are particularly relevant to the job, and reduce or omit other sections. In this way you give the impression to the employer that your skills and experience fit their needs. If, due to constraints of time, you can't meet this ideal of constructing a new CV for each job application, you will have to take particular care that your covering letter draws attention to the relevant aspects of your experience.

You may regard it as slightly dishonest to construct different CVs for different jobs, but this is not so. Most people, and teachers in particular, have acquired a range of skills and undertaken a variety of different tasks during their careers. Given that a CV has to be brief, you must extract the most relevant details from all the possible things you could say about yourself. Instinctively you will 'dress the part' for an interview, choosing the most appropriate set of clothes from your wardrobe, in order to present a certain image of yourself to the interviewer. Constructing a good CV is analogous; all you are doing is presenting your background in such a way that the employer can see you will be able to do the job well. If you feel that you hate the sound of the person you are describing in the CV or on the application form, then you probably should not be applying for the post.

## What does a CV do?

The function of the CV can be stated quite simply: it is to get you an interview. Some professional CV writing firms even refer to the CV as the 'first interview'. In order to fulfil this function, your CV needs to be enticing: it should make the prospective employer realise that you have a suitable background, and that you are an interesting candidate whom they want to meet.

## The presentation of your CV

There are different ways that you can choose to present your CV. An example of clear layout is given in the sample CV on pp.67-8.
  Always consider the following basic points:

● CVs must be typed—handwriting is unacceptable.

● Use good quality white A4 paper. Type on one side only.

● The CV should fit on to two sides of A4 paper.

● Think about layout—you need at least 1 inch margins all around.

● Be consistent with the underlining and capital letters, eg either all sub-headings are underlined or none.

● Start again if there are any visible corrections (although a good correction with correction fluid is not visible on a photocopy).

● Double-check the finished product for spelling mistakes.

● Send a spotless photocopy to the prospective employer and retain the original so you can use it again if necessary.

When you have finished drafting your CV and have typed it up, show it to friends. Get them to comment and suggest how they would improve it.

## If you have had many jobs

Don't give too much detail about each post, particularly if they have been for short periods of time and haven't involved promotion. Try to highlight the differences between the posts to give a plausible rationale for moving frequently, eg: School B—taught French as well as German, or: School B—very large science department offering a wide range of different courses.
  Conversely, if you have had frequent moves due to promotion, then *stress* this information, so that it is clear that you are a high-

achiever, rather than someone who doesn't stick at a job for long.

If you have had a long career, with frequent moves, you may consider summarising all your earlier jobs under a heading *Early Career*, and then give the briefest possible details about these posts, eg:

> Early Career
>
> 1976-77    Mountview School, Berkshire LEA
> Scale 1 Science teacher, fourth-year form tutor.
>
> 1977-78    Hilldale School, Berkshire LEA
> Scale 1 Science teacher. Opportunity to develop
> A-level work. Fourth-year form tutor.
>
> etc

## The content of a CV

When considering the content, bear in mind that your overriding aim is to construct a CV which demonstrates that you can make a definite contribution to the job on offer by showing how you have done so in previous posts.

Your CV should be divided into the following basic headings: personal background, education, career history, voluntary work (if appropriate), additional skills and interests.

The type of information that should be included in your CV can be inferred from reading the sample CV shown on pp.67-8. However, the following points are also worth remembering.

### *Education*
You should include any recent courses that you have taken. A one-day in-service course is not worth mentioning, but courses lasting a half day or an evening a week for a term, or any summer schools that you have attended, should certainly be included, if they are relevant to the post on offer.

### *Career history*
Always start with the most recent job first, and work backwards. For each post include the following information:

● Name of school and LEA (if in the maintained sector)

● Dates of employment

● The nature of your special responsibilities if you are on more than a Scale 1 post. However, use your discretion about mentioning the scale of the post, if you are only on Scale 2.

For a job in education you must mention the scale point, but outside the field, it may be better to omit it, eg 'Head of Biology Department' sounds better than 'Head of Biology — Scale 2'. Similarly, if you are head of a tiny department don't say how many staff you have in the department

- Pastoral responsibilities
- Any major accomplishments and achievements

Try to highlight your skills and experience, and match these to the needs of the employer. Give most detail about your recent post(s) and become progressively briefer the further back you go. It helps if the information is presented in a way which shows a thread of progress running from one job to the next, although you must avoid making it appear rambling.

With your more recent post(s) you will include a brief summary of the job. As a general rule, don't give this information by merely writing down the job title, but instead, aim to phrase it in terms of the results you actually achieved. For example:

| Explanation in terms of job title | Explanation in terms of what you did |
|---|---|
| Pastoral responsibilities — Head of fifth-year. This included developing the pastoral curriculum. | Co-ordinated the pastoral team of six tutors. Developed a life-skills training programme for fifth-year tutor groups. |

*Voluntary work*
Include information about voluntary work on your CV if:

1. It is relevant to the post
2. It involves a consistent commitment on your part over a reasonable length of time. You must feel capable of discussing the work at an interview and demonstrating what experience you gained from carrying it out

*Interests*
Don't fabricate things — you must be able to talk about anything you put down on your CV. If you dream up something really outlandish the employer may decide to do some homework in order to put you through your paces at the interview. Try to choose things which show commitment or an ability to work with others.

*References*
As employers are very unlikely to contact your referees unless you are being seriously considered, it is quite safe to put down the name of your referees on your CV. However, if you are worried about your referees being pestered too much, it is also possible to state 'names and addresses of referees available upon request'.

## Letter of application

Usually you will be asked to send a CV *plus* a letter of application. In the unlikely event that you are asked for a CV only, ignore the advice given earlier in the chapter about always doing what the advert specifies, and send a brief covering letter stating that you have enclosed your CV!

The function of the letter is:

1. To introduce you, and to encourage the employer to read your CV
2. To pick up and develop a few points from your CV in order to demonstrate your suitability for the job

### Content

The overall aim is to inform the employer why you want to work for the organisation and what (in the light of experience derived from your previous posts) you have to offer the employer.

### Paragraph breakdown

You may not want to follow rigidly the structure given below, but it provides a good starting point for drafting the letter.

*Paragraph 1*
Refer to the specific post you are applying for, stating the title of the position given in the advertisement and the vacancy reference number if there is one. You may also want to mention where and when the post was advertised.

*Paragraph 2*
The reasons why you are applying for the post. You may want to mention:

1. In your current job you have been successful at (modestly phrased), and have enjoyed, carrying out similar responsibilities to those of the post on offer

2. Why you want to work for this particular organisation

*Paragraph 3*
Give brief examples of accomplishments in your career which directly relate to the position you seek. Draw attention to important points in your CV which demonstrate the skills and experience required in the post on offer. Include voluntary work experience and any relevant educational qualifications.

Don't say too much:

● Aim to catch the employer's interest — not to provide an autobiography

● Try to fit the letter on to one side of A4 — two at maximum. This will demonstrate to the employer that you can be concise and to the point

● Keep something to talk about at the interview!

## Presentation

If you have good, legible handwriting, then it is better to write by hand. This makes your application distinctive and makes the letter appear more personal.

The layout of the letter is important. Position the letter in the middle of the page with suitable margins all around. Use a block-style of lay-out, ie no indentation. (See sample letter of application on pp.68-9.) Leave some space between 'Yours faithfully' (or 'Yours sincerely' if the letter is written to a named person) and your signature. If the letter is handwritten, print your name underneath the signature.

Finally, always keep a copy of the letter. This can be a photocopy of the actual letter you sent. Or, if you want to keep photocopying costs down, keep your draft for reference.

## Application forms

### Content

The basic factual information required at the beginning of the application form can be taken from the personal data bank. The difficulty lies with the 'narrative' part which tends to lurk at the back of the form. This part comes in a variety of disguises such as 'statement by candidate in support of their application' or 'reasons for applying for this post — and what do you think you can contribute?'.

The advice on how to deal with this narrative section is very similar to that given for writing CVs and letters of application. Think of writing the section as an opportunity to sell yourself. Always aim to demonstrate how your skills and experience match those required for the job. This must be done in a crisp and concise style, rather than being wordy and vague.

Try to fit your answers into the space given on the form. If the space is ludicrously small and you have relevant, pithy information that you think is essential, write 'please see attached sheet' at the bottom of the section on the form. Label the attached sheet clearly, eg:

*Section 5. Further information in support of application—*
*Continued*

Make sure the attached sheet is firmly stapled to the application form. But always ask yourself whether this additional sheet really adds anything to your application.

## Presentation

You should begin by getting a photocopy of the blank application form. Having decided on the content, write the material on this photocopy to see if your layout is suitable. Try to use up the space provided without exceeding it, although as discussed above, this won't always be possible.

It is neater to type out the form, but if the layout of the different sections is complex, it can be extremely difficult to get the typing to fit in the space provided. As an alternative, neat handwriting in black ink is always acceptable.

Finally, keep the rough copy of the form. You will need to read through it when you are invited for an interview.

## Personal data bank

### 1. BACKGROUND INFORMATION

| | |
|---|---|
| *Full Name* | Sarah Holmes |
| *Maiden Name* | Troon |
| *Telephone* | |
| *Number* | Home: Thistown (0123) 56780 |
| | Work: Thistown (0123) 12581 |
| *Date of Birth* | 16.10.58 |
| *Age Last Birthday* | 28 |
| *Marital Status* | Married |

*Ages of Children*
*National Insurance Number*      WD822137E
*DES Number*                     81.52248

## 2. EDUCATION

*(a) SCHOOL*
*(Name of school(s) attended from age 11—with dates)*
Hill Rise School                 1970-1977
*Examinations passed:   (give level (A, O, CSE), subject, grade and dates)*
*O levels:*  1975
English (C), Music (A), Maths (E), Geography (E), Biology (C), Religious Education (A), French (C)
*A levels:*  1977
Religious Education (A), Music (B), English (C)

*Membership of clubs/societies:*
Chair of school Debating Society
Played in orchestra and sang in choir

*Sporting achievements:*
Played in school netball and hockey teams

*(b) COLLEGE/POLYTECHNIC/UNIVERSITY*
*(Name of teacher training college/polytechnic/university attended—with dates)*
1978-1981   Thatown Teacher Training College, Anyshire

*(Title of degree/qualification awarded—with dates)*
1981   BEd II-II Religious Studies
*Main subject:*  Religious Studies
*Subsidiary subject(s):*  Music
*Research project:*  Defining the essential characteristics of Quaker education

*Membership of clubs/societies:   (Give any positions of responsibility)*
College Music Society Orchestra (violin)
College Choir
Informal chamber music (violin)
Accompanying soloists on the piano

*Sporting activities:*  Recreational tennis

*(c) POSTGRADUATE CERTIFICATE OF EDUCATION
(PGCE)*
*(Name of educational institution)*

*(Date PGCE was awarded)*
*(Distinction, or any special award)*
*Main subject:*
*Subsidiary subject:*
*Research project for PGCE course:*

*(d) OTHER POSTGRADUATE QUALIFICATIONS*
*(Name of educational institution)*

*(Title of degree/qualification awarded—with dates)*
*(Distinction or any special awards)*
*Subjects studied:*
*Research component of course:*

*(e) ADDITIONAL TRAINING*
*(Any additional training courses. Include in-service training or
courses taken outside teaching)*

*(For each course state:)*
*Name of organising body:*    National Conference on Inter-
Denominational Education (NCIDE)
*Length of course:*    Two weeks (F/T)
*Subjects covered:*    Teaching Islam
*Date:*    Summer vacation 1984

*(Any further professional qualifications—give dates)*

*(Membership of any professional organisations)*

## 3. EMPLOYMENT

*Current/most recent job:*    Head of Religious Studies
*Date joined/date left:*    September 1983-
*Name of school/college:*    Greenfield School
*Address and telephone number:*    View Road
                                    Thistown
                                    Anyshire H14 9AJ
                                    *Tel:* 0123 12581

*Type of school and number on roll:*    Mixed comprehensive,
1000 on roll

*Scale of post:*    Scale 2

*(If more than Scale 1, give specific responsibilities of the post)*

Head of Religious Studies Department: Two staff in department

*Range of subjects taught: (give course subject, and level at which it was taught)*
Humanities—first- and second-year
Social Studies—CSE/O
Religious Studies—CSE/O/A
Music—practical classes

*Pastoral responsibilities:* First-year form tutor

*Extra-curricular activities:*
Music: support teacher, orchestra and choir
       organised recorder ensemble
Organised speakers for Christian Union and for sixth form
General Studies conference

*Experience of taking pupils on outings/field trips:*
As first-year tutor took tutor group on 10-day annual trip to
Yorkshire
As Head of Religious Studies, organised numerous one-day trips

## SPECIFIC ACHIEVEMENTS

|  | Major Accomplishments | Experience/Skills Acquired |
|---|---|---|
| Production of learning materials | All material in school was written by departmental teams—no text books were used. I wrote the following units:<br>  Religious Feeling,<br>  Town and Village Life<br>  Eskimo Life,<br>  Poverty | • Working closely with other members of the departmental team<br>• Identifying the aims of the course<br>• Writing clear, concise and imaginative learning materials<br>• Completing work according to deadlines |
| Curriculum Development | When I became HOD I introduced a new mode III A level course, which had to be written by the department. This innovatory course led to a great improvement in A level results, and increased the subject from 2 to 15 A level students per year | • Leading department so that new curriculum was successfully implemented<br>• Writing A level course material which was approved by the examining board |

|  | *Major Accomplishments* | *Experience/Skills Acquired* |
| --- | --- | --- |
|  | Introduced new CSE/O level Religious Studies curriculum, replacing the traditional Christianity-based course, with a multi-faith course. This led to a great improvement in CSE/O level results. | ● Providing curricula which were more relevant and engaged the interest of the pupils |
| *Pastoral* | First-year form tutor in charge of a group of 28 first-year pupils | ● Helping pupils adjust to secondary school<br>● Counselling children in my tutor group who were experiencing difficulties<br>● Liaising with other staff and parents when the need arose<br>● Organising group activities and active tutorial work |
| *Managerial* | Head of Department— Religious Studies | ● Responsible for:<br>  curriculum development<br>  staff appointments<br>  staff development, budget<br>● Chairing departmental meetings<br>● Drawing up agenda<br>● Representing department at Heads of Department meetings |
| *Extra-curricular activities* | Support teacher— orchestra and choir | ● Choosing appropriate music<br>● Leading rehearsals<br>● Encouraging pupils to practise music up to performance standard<br>● Organising performances |
| *Outings, Field Trips* | In charge of first-year tutor group on 10-day trip to Yorkshire | ● Leading team of two staff and three sixth form helpers<br>● In charge of 20 12-year-old pupils<br>● Organising day-to-day itinerary<br>● Control of budget |
| *Parent/Teacher* | Regular attendance of PTA meetings | ● Getting on well with a wide range of different people<br>● Developing school/ community links |

*Non-teaching employment:*
*(Include holiday work carried out in college vacations)*

*Name of employer:*    Worked for various employers on a temporary basis
*Duration of work:*    College vacations
*Nature of work:*    Temporary secretarial
*Experience/skills gained from this work:*    Basic office administration

## 4. VOLUNTARY WORK
*(For each voluntary project that you have worked for give:)*
*Name of voluntary organisation:*    Thistown Youth Club
*Length of time associated with the organisation:*    Three years
*Nature of work:*    Voluntary youth leader
*Experience/skills gained from this work:*    Organising sporting and music activities for teenagers aged between 13 and 18

## 5. ADDITIONAL SKILLS
*Foreign language (give level of fluency):*    Basic spoken French
*Secretarial:*    Copy and audio-typing. Experience of working as a secretary
*Word processing:*
*Microcomputing:*
*Driving licence:*    Clean driving licence. Drove school minibus
*Publications: (include articles/letters to newspapers, and any published teaching material)*

## 6. OTHER INTERESTS
*Sports, music, drama or other leisure interests*
*Membership of clubs, societies, music group (state if any offices held)*
Play piano
Regular attender, Friends Meeting House
On children's committee, local Meeting House
On National Quaker Education Committee

## 7. REFERENCES
*(You may want to include more than two names, if you intend to use different referees for different sorts of posts that you are applying for)*

| | |
|---|---|
| *Name:* | Mrs G Williams |
| | Head Teacher |
| | Greenfield School |
| | Thistown |
| | Anyshire H14 9AJ |
| *Tel:* | Thistown (0123) 12581 |
| | |
| *Name:* | Mr R Taylor |
| | Tutor in charge of Religious Studies |
| | Thatown Teacher Training College |
| | Thatown |
| | Anyshire H47 4EE |
| *Tel:* | Thatown (0124) 45961 |
| | |
| *Name:* | Mrs D Smith |
| | Chair, National Quaker Education Committee |
| | 17 Old Street |
| | Thatown |
| | Anyshire H49 2IB |
| *Tel:* | Thatown (0124) 79468 |

## Job specification, sample CV and sample covering letter

A job specification for the post of administrator with a Christian charity is given below. The sample CV and covering letter which follow use the data given in the personal data bank to apply for this post.

### Job specification. Administrator—Christian charity

The person appointed will require:

- Sympathy with the aims of the charity
- Experience of staff and departmental management
- Knowledge and experience of office procedures and administration
- Experience of committee work and procedures
- Experience of conference and holiday planning and administration, and the briefing and debriefing of leaders
- Proven communication skills
- Ability and experience to train others in undertaking speaking and other engagements
- Good liaison and personal relationship skills

CVs, Letters and Application Forms   67

**Sample CV**

CURRICULUM VITAE

| | |
|---|---|
| Name | HOLMES, Sarah Judith |
| Date of Birth | 16.10.58 |
| Place of Birth | Thistown |
| Address | 89 Mistletoe Lane |
| | Thistown |
| | Anyshire HA1 9PD |
| | Tel: Thistown (0123) 56780 |

EDUCATIONAL BACKGROUND

| | |
|---|---|
| 1970-1977 | Hill Rise School, Newtown, Anyshire |
| | A levels: Religious Studies (A), Music (B), English (C) |
| 1978-1981 | Thatown Teacher Training College |
| | Degree: BEd II-II Religious Studies |
| 1984 | Attended annual summer school organised by National Conference on Inter-Denominational Education (NCIDE) |

CAREER HISTORY

| | |
|---|---|
| 1983- | Head of Religious Studies Department Greenfield School (Anyshire LEA) |

Responsible for curricula, staff appointments, staff development, budget and departmental administration.

Developed new Religious Studies curricula for lower school, CSE, O and A level classes. Excellent examination results obtained in all classes.

Organised holidays and outings for groups of pupils.

Arranged guest speakers for Christian Union and sixth form General Studies Conference.

| | |
|---|---|
| 1981-1983 | Religious Studies Teacher Blue House School (Anyshire LEA) |

Taught Religious Studies throughout school up to A level.

Pastoral Responsibility for first-year tutor group.

OTHER INTERESTS

Active member Thistown Friends Meeting House
Committee member of National Quaker Education Committee

REFERENCES

Mrs G Williams
Head Teacher
Greenfield School
View Road
Thistown
Anyshire H14 9AJ
Tel: Thistown (0123) 12581

Mrs D Smith
Chair, National Quaker
Education Committee
17 Old Street
Thatown
Anyshire H49 2IB
Tel: Thatown (0124) 79468

**Sample covering letter**

89 Mistletoe Lane
Thistown
Anyshire HA1 9DP
Tel: (0123) 56780

The Personnel Manager
Goodwill Charity
Goodwill House
Thistown HA1 7EE

1 April, 1986

Dear Sir or Madam

I am applying for the post of administrator advertised in this week's *New Society*.

For the past three years I have been Head of Religious Studies in a large mixed comprehensive school. I have introduced new Religious Studies curricula throughout the school; the size of the A level class has increased from 2 to 15 pupils and the department has obtained an excellent record of CSE, O and A level examination passes. As Head of Department my responsibilities extend beyond the curriculum and include leading my departmental team of teachers, budgeting, staff development, appointing new staff and overall administration of the department. I greatly enjoy the planning and administrative aspects of my post, so I have decided to apply for a job outside teaching which will enable me to develop this type of work.

As Head of Religious Studies I have experience of staff management. I chaired the weekly departmental meetings and represented the department at the school Heads of Department meetings. At

Greenfield School I was in charge of inviting and briefing guest speakers to address Christian Union discussion groups, and sixth form conferences. My background in teaching is an excellent preparation for public speaking and would also help me train others in this area. In addition to teaching experience, I am a trained secretary and always had office jobs during college vacations, so I am familiar with office procedures.

I am very involved in Quaker activities both as a member of Thistown Friends Meeting House, and on the national level, as a representative on the National Quaker Committee on Education. I fully support the aims of the charity.

Please find my CV enclosed.

Yours faithfully


Sarah Holmes

Encl.

*Chapter 5*

# The Interview

When your application form is successful and you are offered an interview, you should always go, even if you are now doubtful whether you actually want the job, or you think your chances of getting it are extremely slim. Any interview will allow you to practise and develop your interview skills, thereby increasing your confidence. In addition, an interview provides an invaluable opportunity to find out more about careers in the field.

## Pre-interview preparation

### Find out about the employer

It is vital to find out as much as you can about the employer. When you bring this knowledge to the interview, both in the answers you give and the questions you raise, you will be able to demonstrate your commitment, interest and motivation to the employer. Being well prepared in this way will also help you to feel more confident in the interview, which in turn enables you to create a better impression. On the other side of the coin, your pre-interview research may lead you to discover that the employer as an organisation doesn't appeal to you, or that it is in financial difficulties and is currently shedding many employees. This research may stop you from landing yourself in a job which you dislike, or in a job which does a disappearing trick on you in a few months' time.

To guide your information search, try to put yourself on the other side of the desk and imagine the questions the employer is likely to ask you. You may even want to consult the Institute of Personnel Management's Code of Practice for Interviewers to help you to see the interview from the interviewer's point of view. Free copies of the code, with additional comments, are available if you send a self-addressed envelope to:

The Institute of Personnel Management
Camp Road
London SW19 4UW

Divide the information that you are finding out about the employer into different categories. The list below is not intended to be exhaustive; furthermore, some of the points are more directly applicable to industry, although many of them also apply to work in other areas, such as the voluntary sector. Armed with the job description that the employer has sent, you should go through the list to extract the relevant questions.

*(a) Financial aspects of the employer*
Who owns or finances the employer. Profitability. Turnover. Any recent take-over attempts. Number of branches, divisions or subsidiaries.

*(b) Products/services supplied by the employer*
What products/services are supplied. Reputation in the field. How the employer compares with competitors/other organisations in terms of reputation, size, profitability. What the retail outlets are. How products/services are advertised. The role of PR. Problems with production/supply of products and services.

*(c) Structure of the organisation*
Number of employees. Names of the senior personnel. Staff turnover. Prospects for internal promotion. Any recent redundancies. Who the post-holder will report to. Why the post is vacant. How long the previous incumbent held the job.

*(d) Plans for the future*
Any plans to expand the range of products/services supplied. The significance of any recent technological developments. Recent shifts in policy.

*(e) General information*
General economic trends. The state of the industry/trade/profession. Significance of any recent changes in legislation.

### Where do you find this information?

1. The principal source of information will be the company or organisation itself. Write to or telephone the PR Department, and ask for any recent press releases, promotional information or a copy of the company newspaper to be sent to you. For a public limited company, write to the company secretary, and ask for a copy of the Annual Report and

Accounts. From this you will be able to find out about the recent performance of the company, future planning, whether the number of employees is stable and a detailed breakdown of different divisions in the company. Government bodies, and many other organisations in the voluntary sector, including charities, also publish Annual Reports.

2. In large cities, the public reference library will contain a number of different directories and publications which provide information about the company or organisation. Useful publications to consult are given in Appendix 1. If for some reason you find that the particular organisation you are interested in is not covered in the reference library, the librarian may be willing to make further enquiries for you.

## What you have to offer the employer

No employer will want to employ a reject or a non-coper from another profession. It is therefore essential that you work out a plausible, positive reason for wishing to leave teaching. When asked by the employer why you are changing career, don't say that you are fed up with poor classroom discipline or that the low status of the job and the drudgery of marking are getting you down. These may well be the real reasons why you want to change career, but you must not let the employer sense that this is so. Instead of phrasing your answer in terms of the negative 'push' factors out of teaching tell the employer about the positive 'pull' factors towards the job in question. For example:

| *Question* | *Answer* |
| --- | --- |
| Why are you intending to leave teaching and applying for this post as: | |
| (a) a trainee manager? | As a head of department I had responsibility for the Science Department. Not only was I responsible for choosing the science curriculum used throughout the school, but I also managed the department in terms of staff appointments. I greatly enjoyed the managerial aspects of the job, and that is why I am applying for this post. |

| *Question* | *Answer* |
|---|---|
| (b) a trainee counsellor? | As a teacher in a large comprehensive school I had pastoral responsibility for a group of fifth-year pupils. It was very stimulating to get to know this group of pupils, and help them to decide on their future plans. I found the pastoral aspects of the job were the most rewarding, and that is why I am keen to change direction and train as a counsellor. |
| (c) an employee in an international importing company? | I originally went into teaching because of my love of languages and this love has remained with me. Although I enjoy being a teacher, I would like greater opportunity to speak French at the high standard demanded by this job, and to travel frequently to France. |

In your pre-interview preparation you must also work out how to reply when the interviewer questions you about the relevance of your teaching experience. As a candidate who is in the process of changing career direction you are a more risky choice than someone who is in that profession already. You must compensate for this initial disadvantage by your ability to give confident answers, showing precisely how your background in teaching is relevant to the job in question. Any lack of self-confidence, or vague woolly answers will leave the employer unconvinced. You must be prepared to answer questions about the relevance of your previous experience as it is probably the employer's foremost concern. In the unlikely event of the employer not raising this question, you will have to bring it up yourself! Whenever this issue is discussed, you must always remember the basic principle: never say you are *just* a teacher, but instead say that *because* of your background in teaching you have acquired a large repertoire of different skills that will enable you to do the job.

For example, a secondary school biology teacher, when interviewed for a place on a research project to study for a PhD, responded in the following way:

> I pointed out that many of the skills required in teaching such as organisation, self-discipline and creativity, were essential for carrying out scientific research.

A secondary school maths teacher, now working in computing, had this to say of her interview:

> I emphasised the managerial aspects of the job, for example leading a team of tutors, dealing with parents, and contacting outside agencies. I also stressed the variety of responsibilities one has in addition to classroom teaching, like organising a week-long trip for the first-years involving 170 pupils, 13 staff and a budget of £10 000.

As discussed in the previous chapter, when you were filling in the application form you used information contained in the job description and any further details the organisation sent you to work out what sort of skills and experiences the ideal candidate should have. You then went through your CV and listed those experiences, in both paid employment and in voluntary work, which matched the requirements of the job description.

The employer must have been impressed by your application form and thought that you had a suitable background for the job, because they have offered you an interview. After all, if they thought that your background in teaching was totally irrelevant to the job in question, you wouldn't have been shortlisted. The task of the interview is to convert this initial interest which the employer has shown in you, into the realisation on their part that you are the person for the job.

But you must also realise that, however stunning your application form is, you will never be offered a job on the basis of the form alone. You should see filling in the application form as getting a foot in the door—it provides you with access to the next stage; the interview itself is the decisive challenge. You must always be prepared to discuss and enlarge upon any of the points you mentioned in the application form or CV. For example, imagine a situation where the job description said that the ability to work as part of a team was important, and you mentioned in your application form that your school department was organised on a team basis. As part of the pre-interview preparation you must think about the sort of follow-up questions that the interviewer may pursue, such as how many people were in each team, how the different jobs in the team were allocated, and whether it was a successful form of organisation. Your application form should be thought of as an 'invitation' to discuss any of the points raised on it, and you must ensure that you are fully prepared to take part in this discussion.

There are also some aspects of pre-interview preparation which apply to any candidate, not just to the career-changing teacher. If there are gaps in your CV or if you have ever stepped down or sideways, you will probably be questioned about it. Tackle these questions in a positive way, for example discussing the actual advantages of a sideways move to a different school and how this move has helped your career in the long run. Avoid giving any negative reasons, even if they are true. It is far better to say that you moved sideways because the second school had a larger department, and offered more promotion opportunities, even if the actual reason was that your head of department was an intolerable work-shy bigot, or discipline in the first school was so bad that you feared for your safety!

## The interview itself

As a teacher you must already have had the experience of being interviewed. I am therefore assuming that information on *basic* interviewing skills, such as the necessity of arriving on time, and dressing appropriately, would be superfluous. However, if you feel that you could do with brushing up on the basics, then consult *Getting a New Job* (1981), published by the Consumers' Association.

### Teachers are experienced interviewees

The prospect of an interview for a job in an entirely new field probably seems very daunting. The more you want the job, the more ill at ease you are likely to feel. But if you stand back for a minute and reflect on your experiences as a teacher, you will soon realise that you are extremely well equipped to deal with any interview.

First of all, think about the interviews you have had for teaching posts. These must be among the most taxing interviews devised by mankind. Teaching interviews are particularly stressful. With many other jobs you will only be interviewed for an hour or two, and then asked back for a further interview on a different day, if the employer is still interested. Teaching interviews, however, are usually half-day or whole-day affairs. And this is just the beginning of the story!

In an interview for a non-teaching post you may only have to face two or three people on the other side of the desk. Conversely, teaching interviews are usually panel affairs. Being interviewed by a panel is much more daunting than facing only two or three strange faces. Questions may come from different members of the panel in rapid succession, and you have the difficult task of holding on to all this information, while deciding whom to answer first. Panel interviews also pose the problem of how to keep all the different members of the panel interested and involved in what you are saying. You have to attempt to answer the person who has posed the question, while remaining in eye contact with the other members of the panel.

But these are not the only stresses of the teaching interview. Because teaching interviews usually involve a panel, all of the candidates tend to be seen on the same day, so that the panel does not have to reconvene at a later date. Most people find group interviews particularly difficult. It is hard enough to maintain an aura of confidence and charm when you are faced with complete strangers on the other side of the desk firing penetrating questions at you. It is virtually impossible not to feel like giving up and walking out of the interview when you are interviewed as a collective. Invariably the other candidates appear to be more intelligent, witty and experienced and seem to have an ability to dream up answers that you wished you had thought of. Furthermore, if the group interview involves having a group discussion among yourselves while the members of the interviewing panel listen in the background, you have to walk on a tightrope, balancing the necessity of appearing critical and perceptive on the one hand, against the danger of assassinating the other candidates, and therefore seeming to be unnecessarily aggressive, on the other.

As a teacher being interviewed for a non-teaching post, you may imagine that the range of topics that you could be questioned on is too enormous to manage. However, think back to teaching interviews that you have had in the past. In a typical teaching interview you may be asked about anything from detailed factual questions on your subject from the head of department, to questions about the latest pedagogical theories from the head, and from questions about child development from the pastoral staff, to questions aimed at uncovering aspects of your personality: all this in an attempt to see if you will fit in with the overall ethos of the school.

There is one final stress of a teaching interview that is worth considering. In an interview for a job as a publisher you won't be faced with booksellers, or members of the book-buying public. Similarly, in an interview for a job as a social worker, you won't have face-to-face contact with needy clients. But in a teaching interview, not only will you be interviewed by a large panel, you will also have contact with the pupils. It is extremely hard to know how to react to comments from pupils such as, 'Are you strict?', or 'Can we muck around in your classes?', when you are being shepherded around the school by a member of the staff.

I hope I have convinced you that the experience gained from teaching interviews provides an excellent grounding in interview skills. If you have survived and succeeded in the assault course of teaching interviews, then an interview for a non-teaching post may well seem like a relaxed amble in comparison.

There is another reason why teachers deserve to have confidence in their ability to excel at interviews. The most important skill that you need in order to be a first-rate interviewee is the ability to listen, and to pick up the cues that the interviewer gives about the sort of person he or she envisages for the job. A good interviewee uses the feedback from the interviewer to put forward a picture of herself that accords with the person she feels that the interviewer is looking for. To give a concrete example, the interviewer may pose a series of questions concerning the candidate's ability to work under pressure, and to complete open-ended tasks. The sensitive interviewee may realise that underlying these questions is an attempt to find out if the candidate can stick to deadlines. She then replies, not by specifically stating that she is good at sticking to deadlines, but by giving concrete examples of work that has been successfully completed according to a tight schedule.

This process of using cues from the interviewer to build up a picture of the ideal candidate, and then displaying aspects of oneself that mirror this ideal, can take place quite unconsciously. Skilled interviewees may be quite unaware that this is what they are doing. However, the process of being sensitive to what other people are saying, and altering one's behaviour in the light of this information, has become almost instinctive to any teacher. On numerous occasions I have walked into a classroom, intending to begin with a brief, punchy explanation of some practical work, so that the class will get on with carrying out the experiment themselves; I have sensed, though, that the class is buzzing with excitement — perhaps there has been a fight in the playground, or a pupil has had a dramatic confrontation with a member of staff in a previous lesson. I have had to abandon my original lesson strategy and begin by giving the class some written work that would calm them down, before they could attempt any practical work. To survive in the classroom you need to pick up cues from the 20 to 30 other individuals, and adjust your behaviour accordingly. Surviving an interview, where one has to face only two or three people, is a walk-over in comparison.

Above all, remember that every successful lesson you teach involves selling a product (your subject) and selling yourself, to an often unwilling audience. Good teachers become adept at presenting themselves as determined, businesslike, yet pleasant individuals. If you demonstrate these same qualities at an interview, you are very likely to succeed.

A word of warning! Teachers have a reputation for being bossy and for finding it difficult to 'switch off' once they come home. Although this stereotype is probably unjustified, it is worth bearing in mind that interviewers won't appreciate an overtly domineering manner.

## How to convince the employer of your suitability

There is no set formula guaranteeing success in an interview, and different careers experts may offer conflicting advice. For example, some experts advise you to prepare a list of the questions you want to ask but leave the actual list at home, whereas others say bring the list with you, in order to show the interviewer that you are well prepared. I prefer the former strategy, but I have used this example to illustrate that different experts have markedly different opinions.

Most experts, however, would agree with the general point that at an interview you should be natural, lively and above all try to imagine yourself in the position of the interviewer. This enables you to build up a picture of the sort of person the interviewer is seeking, and to present aspects of yourself which match this image.

Richard Nelson Bolles, in *What Colour is Your Parachute?*, elaborates on this point:

> You must show this person (the interviewer) how your skills can help them with their problems *as they perceive them*. I cannot stress this strongly enough. You may think you perceive a problem that they are absolutely blind to, in that organisation; but if so, you are going to have to delicately and very skillfully explore how they perceive that particular problem area, before you hit them over the head with your brilliant insight into it all.

It is also worth remembering that the job does not always go to the best qualified candidate, but may go to the person who will best fit in with the rest of the team. Compared to other candidates who have not switched career, you may be lacking in formal relevant qualifications for the post. But if you present yourself in a really positive light and show you are the sort of person who is committed, works well with other people and manages to get the task completed, you may find that you are offered the job.

## Convince the employer that your background in teaching counts

This is the most important task for you to accomplish in the interview. It may not be good enough for the employer to see you as an intelligent, hard-working likeable person. You have to convince him that even though your background is in teaching, many of the skills acquired as a teacher are directly relevant to the post on offer.

Your pre-interview research is important here. Combining a careful reading of the job description with the background information on the organisation has enabled you to build up a clear picture of the qualities and skills that the post-holder will need. You are then in a position to relate these skills to skills you have learnt through being a teacher.

When the interviewer challenges you on the relevance or limitations of your background, try to make him identify the specific qualities that you are seen to lack. For example:

*Interviewer:*    You have an excellent background to work in the educational field, but I am unsure about the relevance of this background to the post we have to offer.

*Candidate:*    In what particular ways do you feel that I may be lacking, given my background in education?

Once the interviewer specifies exactly where he sees the difficulty lies, you are in a good position to show him how you do possess the necessary skills.

For example:

*Interviewer:*    I don't doubt your ability to teach your subject, but how does your background enable you to write creative advertising copy to very tight deadlines?

*Candidate:*    Well, working to deadlines is no problem. As a teacher I am experienced at planning lessons according to a rigid deadline. I can hardly tell a class to talk quietly among themselves for an hour as I didn't have time to prepare their lesson the previous night. As for creativity, teaching is

> an essentially creative process. You have to
> prepare a wide range of materials which will
> catch the interest of pupils of different ages and
> abilities. In fact, teaching isn't unlike writing
> copy, as I am constantly trying to sell my
> subject to the pupils!

In most situations, particularly if you have carefully prepared for the interview, you should be able to make some link between the skills needed for the job on offer, and the skills you have gained from working as a teacher. But it is still possible that the interviewer will challenge your experience in such a way that you can't find any relevant link.

*Interviewer:*   As a trainee social worker you will need a
                 knowledge of the relevant legislation. I don't see
                 how your background in teaching will help you.

In this situation, *briefly* acknowledge the truth of what the interviewer is saying, but then go on to give concrete examples showing how you are eager and adept at learning new skills. For example:

*Candidate:*   I agree that I have no knowledge of the
               relevant legislation, but throughout my teaching
               career I have had to develop and widen my
               skills, and I am a quick learner! To give you an
               example, I trained as a maths teacher, and I had
               very little computer experience. But in my third
               year of teaching, the school bought 10 micro-
               computers. I attended an evening computer
               course on a weekly basis for a term, and I was
               then able to teach computer studies throughout
               the school.

By acknowledging your initial limitation, you show that you are honest, and that you have a good understanding of what the job on offer entails. The second part of your answer then demonstrates that you are serious and committed to your work, and that you have the ability to learn new skills.

Another way that the interviewer may approach the issue of the relevance of your background is to ask a series of questions aimed at finding out how you would cope with a particular situation.

*Interviewer:*   You are applying for a post in the Personnel
                 Department. One of the tasks of this department
                 is to negotiate with the unions. What would you

> do when a shop steward comes to see you, threat-
> ening industrial action if new technology, which
> will result in job losses, is installed in the plant?

If you have done your pre-interview preparation adequately, you shouldn't be surprised at this question. Careful analysis of the job description would have shown you that negotiating with the unions was an important part of the department's work. Your detailed research on the state of the industry, and on the future plans of the company, would have alerted you to this issue of new technology. In your answer you need to distinguish between those skills you already possess, and those that you will need to gain in order to do the job on offer.

*Candidate:*     From the job description that you sent me, I
realised that negotiating with the unions was an
important part of the job. Successful industrial
relations depend upon skills such as honesty,
being able to deal with a wide range of people,
and seeing an issue from two different points of
view. These are three skills that I have had to
develop to survive as a classroom teacher.
However, the job would also require me to know
about the relative advantages and
disadvantages of the new technology, any health
and safety considerations, and the legislation
governing industrial action and redundancies. I
would welcome the opportunity to learn about
these further aspects if I was offered the job.

In this answer you reassure the interviewer that you do possess many of the necessary skills, and you also demonstrate that you have a realistic notion of what the job in the personnel department entails.

Another useful strategy to adopt if the interviewer questions the relevance of your teaching experience is to turn the roles around, and ask him what he knows about teaching. This obviously has to be done carefully, as you don't want to appear to be over-aggressive, or on the defensive. However, many older people have little idea of what teaching today involves, as they have an image of school life derived from their own schooldays, which may be far removed from the reality of school life now. Politely but firmly ask the interviewer if he realises how stressful school teaching can be, and give examples of some of the pressures of the job.

In this way you may show the prospective employer that teaching is not the 'doddle' that many people who know nothing about the profession assume, and that in order to cope in the classroom, teachers have to possess skills such as tact, firmness and the ability to think on their feet.

## How to respond to difficult questions

If it is a difficult question, but you think you can answer it, give yourself extra time by saying something like, 'That's an interesting question. Can I think about it for a moment?'. This will give you a few extra seconds to organise your response.

If you are unsure why the interviewer is asking the question, you could consider saying, 'I could answer the question better if I knew why you were asking that', or 'How does the question relate to the job?'. If the interviewer elaborates on the question it will enable you to give a more precise and relevant answer.

If you find a question ambiguous, then ask for clarification, rather than ploughing on regardless, and then realising half-way through that you have entirely missed the point of the question. It doesn't do any harm to display reasonable caution, and show that you like things to be clarified.

If you really don't know how to answer a question, or if your mind suddenly becomes a complete blank, then say so. To waffle on, when it is clear to both you and the interviewer that you haven't a clue what you are talking about, is much more damaging to your chances.

## When the going gets tough

In a panel interview, you may find that you are subjected to a rapid machine-gun fire of questions. Each question is posed so quickly that you haven't had time to answer one, before the next one comes along. In this situation, pass the responsibility back to the panel by saying, 'You have asked a number of different questions. Which one would you like me to answer first?'. In this way you also demonstrate to the panel that you are able to keep calm, even when placed under pressure.

An alternative tactic that the interviewer might adopt is to try to make you angry. Although the interviewer may be behaving in this way because he is a naturally rude individual, it is more likely that he is trying to find out how you react to pressure. He may also be on the look-out to see if this pressure results in you changing the story about the factual content of your CV or application form, in order to check the truth of details that you provided.

As an experienced teacher you have often had to deal with children whose main aim in life is to wind up the teacher. You know that the only solution is to adopt a calm but firm approach, and that you must never let the pupils think that they are succeeding in making you annoyed. This is the stance that you have to adopt if the interviewer tries to needle you by making fun of your answers, or by misrepresenting what you have said. Correct the interviewer firmly, or perhaps re-state your own point of view, in order to show that you can handle pressure, but never indicate that you are upset or angry.

## How to deal with questions about money

In teaching, posts are offered at particular scale points, and your salary is therefore not negotiable, except in the comparatively rare cases where the scale point itself may depend on the experience of the successful candidate. Outside teaching you may apply for a post where the advertisement states that the 'salary is negotiable depending on age and experience', or a wide salary range may be quoted in the advertisement. Teachers find it difficult to accept the idea that salaries can be quite flexible, and they have little experience in the delicate intricacies of salary negotiations.

## How to negotiate a salary successfully

Don't ask about the salary too early on in the interview, as you want to give the impression that you are more concerned with finding out about the responsibilities of the post than the remuneration. If the employer tries to get you to say what salary you are looking for, ask to return to the matter later, when you have a clearer picture of what the job entails. If the interviewer continues to press the point, turn it round, and ask what salary range they had in mind.

Once the interviewer has stated the range, you should aim to negotiate. This has to be done very skilfully and tactfully. Ask too high a price, and the employer will go to another candidate. But if you aim too low, you will make the employer think that there is something wrong with you, and that you don't know the current salary range of the industry, or that you are absolutely desperate to get any job.

If the firm suggest a salary range of £13 000-£17 000, they will try at first to fill the post at the lowest salary range. But in practice they will be quite willing to go up to the midway point. In order to negotiate successfully, you need to find out what the current post-holder earns. The firm may well try to tell you about salaries on first appointment, but try to extract the actual current salary of the post-holder.

One of the main reasons why people leave teaching is the low salaries compared to other professions. The interviewer knows this, and will try to get you to disclose your present salary, in order to use this as a starting point for discussion. If at all possible, don't fall into this trap. Tactfully but firmly point out that they are offering a post outside the teaching field, and therefore what is relevant is the salary scale usually adopted in this field, rather than your teaching salary.

If the interviewer is determined to extract your current salary, don't lie and claim that you have a higher salary than you actually do. If you are a teacher being paid on the Burnham scale, it is easy for the employer to discover your basic salary. Moreover, if you are offered and you accept the job, your previous salary can be found out from your P45 and P60 tax forms.

Don't try to negotiate a suitable salary before you have had a firm offer of the job. You need to be sure that you are the person they want, as you are then in a much stronger position. In order to decide if the salary on offer is acceptable, you need to consider other points besides the basic salary itself:

● Opportunities for promotion and training
● The date of the next salary review
● The hours of work
● The amount of holiday
● Pension schemes
● Benefits such as a car or expenses
● Overtime payments

You shouldn't make any firm decision about accepting the post until you have had information on all of these points.

If the employer offers you the job at the interview, don't rush into making a final decision there and then. The employer will usually give you a day or two to consider the offer and to discuss it with your family. You must use your own judgement on this point.

You may feel that the salary on offer is lower than you had hoped. In this situation, suggest to the employer that the salary is reviewed in three or six months' time. Alternatively, you may try to negotiate for extra benefits such as a company car or a pay bonus scheme. Only you can decide if it is wise to try to improve the employer's offer when you return with your answer. In general, you are unlikely to be successful if you ask for anything other than minor changes to the salary and fringe benefits package.

Discussions about money are difficult, particularly for the teacher who has had little experience of these matters. However, don't let your natural disinclination to talk about money result in your accepting the employer's suggestion that they will write and confirm that they are offering you the job, and that they will state the salary on offer in this letter. Once you are in this situation you have no room to manoeuvre, as you either have to write back and accept the job with the terms on offer, or refuse the job unless the pay package is improved. In the latter case, the employer is likely either to offer the job to the second choice, or to withdraw the offer if the job is not accepted on the terms stated in the letter.

Skilful money negotiations are hard to carry out. But if you use the combination of tact and firmness which you have developed as a teacher, you should be able to arrive at a pay package which is acceptable to both you and your employer.

## Questions you should ask

Just as there are no set answers you can learn off by heart that will see you through any interview, there are no set questions which will always be applicable. It is a good idea to prepare for the interview by thinking about questions that you want to ask, but don't learn these off pat.

Bear in mind that if you are being interviewed for a job with a large organisation, you may have a preliminary meeting with someone from the personnel department who will give you background information about the organisation before you have your main interview for the job. In this situation you might find that the personnel department provide answers to some of the questions that you had planned to ask in your interview.

Many questions will occur to you in the course of your discussion with the interviewer. When they do, ask them then and there, rather than waiting until the end, when the employer usually asks you if you have any questions. By involving the interviewer in this way, you convert the interview into a dialogue. The employer is much more likely to enjoy the interview, and to see you in a positive light. Throughout the interview ask the interviewer to expand on points that he has raised. This will help you to change the interview from a one-way firing line into a two-way discussion.

There are a number of general points to consider. First, try to ask questions which show your grasp of the job, and of the field as a whole. From your pre-interview preparation you should have a good idea of the specific concerns and goals of the organisation. Ask about these issues. Be as specific as possible in these questions, thereby demonstrating your background knowledge of the organisation. Avoid vague, woolly questions which could apply to any job. Second, ask questions that require more than a yes/no answer, so that the questions will engage the interviewer in discussion. Third, avoid questions that have already been answered in the literature that the company has sent you. Finally, you should always try to ask questions that show you have thought analytically about the job, and which demonstrate that you are capable of identifying possible areas of strength and weakness in the organisation.

The list below contains some examples of good questions. Obviously, you will have to modify them so that they are directly applicable to the post on offer.

- Is this a new position? If not, what has happened to the previous post-holder, and how long did he hold the post?
- Where does this position fit into the structure of the organisation as a whole?
- Who would be my immediate supervisor if I were offered the post?
- What are the prospects for internal promotion?
- If you could change one thing in this department/company/ organisation, what would it be? (Even the most experienced interviewer will probably have to hesitate when asked this question. The answer may also bring to the surface any problems that exist in the organisation)
- What does it take to succeed in this post? (As the interviewer lists the qualities and experience of the ideal employee, you can mentally scan your own CV and make sure that you subtly refer to these characteristics in your subsequent answers. Conversely, if the person he describes is anathema to you, it should alert you to the fact that you are unlikely to be happy in this organisation)

Some careers experts advise candidates to conclude the interview by asking a question such as, 'Have you any reservations about my doing the job?', or 'Does my experience seem to be what you are looking for?'. You certainly have to be full of self-confidence to do this, and many people may not feel happy about being so pushy. If this sort of question doesn't appeal to you, don't ask it. But if you feel happy with it, then there may be some advantages to be gained.

The most common response from the interviewer is that there are still other candidates to be interviewed. You can respond to this by saying, 'I appreciate that but I hoped that you would clarify the position as far as I was concerned.'

If the interviewer then replies to your question and lists some of the reservations she or he has, you may well be able to put forward some further examples to show that you do possess the necessary qualities and experience. Moreover, by asking this question, and receiving a frank answer, you have the advantage of leaving the room with a good picture of where you stand.

Finally, you should never leave the interview without asking when you can expect to hear a final decision from the employer.

## Getting some interview practice

If you think that you need some practice at being interviewed, you may consider being an interviewee in a role-play. The Institute of Personnel Management runs short courses training personnel managers in how to become good interviewers. For these courses they occasionally need people to sit on the other side of the desk and act the role of the interviewee. This would give you an opportunity to be interviewed by a panel and afterwards you would receive some feedback about how you did. The courses are held in Central London and the interviewee is required to attend for a whole morning. If you are interested in taking part in such a role-play, contact:

The Course and Conference Department
The Institute of Personnel Management
IPM House
Camp Road
London SW19 4UW
*Tel:* 01-946 9100

## Claiming expenses

Always accept when the employer offers to pay the expenses you have incurred in attending the interview. Accepting expenses will never harm your chances of being offered the post. In order to make it easy for the employer to reimburse you, be prepared with the information necessary to fill in the claim form. This will be public transport costs, or mileage if you came by car.

If possible, give your claim form to a secretary, rather than to the person who is actually interviewing you. Furthermore, don't raise the question of expenses during the middle of the interview, as the interviewer is likely to perceive it as a distraction. The employer may tell you beforehand that they do not pay expenses. If you are unemployed it may be worth finding out if the MSC will reimburse you for the cost of the return fare. Ask for leaflet EPL66 at your nearest Jobcentre.

## References

When you are applying for a teaching post, the employer usually takes up your references prior to the interview. However, outside teaching this practice is not common. It is more usual for the employer to contact the references after you have been offered the job, with the understanding that the job offer is subject to the references being satisfactory. For non-teaching posts it is acceptable for you to withhold the names of your referees until you have actually been offered the job.

Choose your references carefully. One of the referees must be somebody who can comment on your work. As a teacher, this means that you have to use the head teacher of your current school, or the head teacher of your last school, if you are unemployed. The head teacher should always be cited in favour of the head of department. If you don't use the head teacher as a referee the employer will want to find out why, and this may count against you.

Quite often you will be asked to provide two references. This means that in addition to the head teacher you can use your supervisor from college/university, or, if you have done any voluntary or vacation work which is relevant to the post on offer, you could use someone who knows your work in this capacity.

You want the referees to be as favourably disposed towards you as possible, so use your tact. Always give advance warning to your referees that you have used their name, and mention that they may be telephoned or written to regarding your application. Nobody, including referees, likes to be caught unprepared, and if a prospective employer telephones them out of the blue, they are unlikely to be too pleased. You should also give the referees some brief details about the job, and why you are interested in it. This will enable them to structure their reference in the light of this information, rather than giving you a vague reference which could apply to any job.

It is a good idea to write and thank your referees for their assistance, when you are offered a job. As their references have helped you to get the job, it is courteous to keep them informed. This also sustains their involvement and interest in your career plans, and ensures that if you need to ask them for a reference in future, they will be happy to oblige.

## After the interview

Interviews for teaching are unusual. The final decision is made on the day of the interview, so the candidates leave the interview knowing whether they have been successful or not. This rarely happens outside the teaching profession, and candidates may have to wait for a few weeks before they are informed of the outcome of the interview.

As soon as possible after the interview, make a few brief notes on how the interview went. Write down the name and position of the person who interviewed you, note any questions that you think you answered particularly well, or particularly badly, and any important questions that you raised in the interview, together with how these questions were received. If you are offered a second interview these notes will enable you to avoid asking the same questions twice. Alternatively, if your interview proves to be unsuccessful, the notes may help you to understand what went wrong.

At the interview the employer should have given some indication about when they will get back in contact with you. If the time period that the employer mentioned has elapsed, telephone the personnel department, and ask when you can hope to hear their final decision. As long as you are polite, persistence of this kind will do no harm, and will merely demonstrate your commitment and interest in the post.

Even if the employer has made a verbal offer of the job at the interview, always wait for written confirmation before you hand in your notice to your current employer. When you receive this confirmation, if you want to accept the post, first telephone the employer to inform them of your decision, and then write a letter of confirmation.

If you decide to decline the offer, write to the employer giving a reason for this decision. It is worth taking the time to write a good letter, offering a plausible reason, even if it is not perhaps the major reason underlying your choice. Remember that you may want to apply for another post within the organisation at a future date, and that many industries and professions are quite small, and employers exchange information between themselves.

If the eventual outcome is unsuccessful and the employer informs you that you have not got the post, resist the temptation to throw away all correspondence, interview notes, and forms relating to the job. As I pointed out above, you may want to apply for a post with the same organisation in the future, and you would find it useful to remind yourself who interviewed you, and some of the questions they asked. Also, it is likely that you will apply for another post in the same field, and filling in the next application form will be much easier if you have kept other earlier attempts. Finally, by analysing the unsuccessful application form and interview notes, you may be able to throw some light on why your application failed. This will help you with applications that you make in future.

*Chapter 6*

# Re-training and Self-employment

One option open to you, when you are considering leaving the teaching profession, is to go back to your books and re-train for another career. But 're-training' is a very broad concept—a point clearly illustrated by the sample of 50 ex-teachers interviewed for this book. Almost two-thirds of the sample undertook some form of re-training. However, don't jump to the conclusion that leaving teaching means the inevitable approach of years of late nights spent swotting, valiantly sipping cups of black coffee to keep yourself awake. Admittedly there were a few ex-teachers who opted for full-time training courses which lasted over a year (a research scientist, an architect and a clinical psychologist), but the sample also included people whose re-training took one year (a careers adviser, a drama therapist and an educational psychologist), less than a year (the many ex-teachers who took three- or four-month MSC-funded computer training schemes) and also ex-teachers who didn't return to college, but were provided with on-the-job re-training by the company that employed them. A number of art teachers who went into graphic design built up their portfolios at evening classes and classes at their local teachers' centres. Finally, about a third of the sample, including a journalist, a publisher and an actor, received no formal re-training whatsoever.

As there are so many different training courses that might be relevant to the career-changing teacher, it would be impossible to include details of every course in this book. Instead, in this chapter I discuss some of the questions that you need to ask yourself *before* you embark on re-training, and go on to consider a number of organisations and reference sources that you can consult, to find your way through the maze of training provision.

## Do I have to re-train?

You must begin by asking yourself this question. Obviously the answer depends to a large extent on the particular career you have decided to pursue, as well as on the level at which you intend to enter it. In some cases embarking on a full-time academic re-training course might be the only option, eg if you want to work as a speech therapist or remedial gymnast. In other cases, such as personnel management, you can choose between studying full or part time at a college, or even studying for the exams at home using a correspondence course. You must also realise that in certain careers there will be alternatives to embarking on an examination-based training course. For example, in the field of computing you might have to decide between a fairly academic postgraduate masters/diploma course, or receiving on-the-job training on a graduate traineeship scheme. The former choice might not always lead to better career prospects.

The decision to embark on a full-time course which will take a period of years clearly requires more careful consideration than the decision to take a short part-time evening course. But whatever the course duration or level of study, push yourself to answer the question 'Will studying this course really help me with my career plans?'. Acquiring so many qualifications that you add a complete alphabet of letters after your name won't necessarily get you job satisfaction—or even a job.

Of course, all teachers know that not all studying need be vocationally orientated. Learning for the pure pleasure of learning is admirable, as long as you are clear that this is the case from the outset. What you must avoid is choosing a course in order to help you with your career, only to find that the course is not recognised as a useful qualification.

## How to find out if the course is necessary/useful

If you *have* to possess a qualification in order to practise in your new career, then the relevant professional association will have all the information about which particular training courses are recognised, and whether it is possible to gain the qualification through a part-time or correspondence course.

The problem arises in careers where a particular qualification may be useful, but is not absolutely essential. For example, if you want to move from classroom teaching into museum education you might consider studying for a postgraduate diploma or degree in museum studies. This qualification might be helpful, but it is not an essential prerequisite for all jobs in the field of museum education. In this situation you need to do two things. First, write to the relevant professional association (in this case the Museums Association) and ask them whether they think you would be better advised to take the course, or look for a museum post where on-the-job training would be obtained. Second, ask your contact(s) in the field if the course you had in mind is viewed favourably and if they think taking the course would improve your job prospects.

## Is complete re-training feasible?

You need to be a positive-thinking realist when answering this question. In general, people are narrow-minded in their views about career changes and adopt the attitude that once you're 30 it's much too late. I think that anything is possible! Even medical schools claim to consider students up to the age of 30 (although in practice many tend to impose a limit of 25), and my sample of ex-teachers included a 30-year old woman who had six further years training as an architect in front of her!

In other areas, such as training as social workers, mature entrants with relevant experience are positively encouraged to apply. In fact, some Certificate of Qualification in Social Work (CQSW) courses have *minimum* ages at which you can apply. In reality though, it is necessary to temper this 'anything is possible' enthusiasm with a few unpleasant but true provisos. You have to consider the three Cs: Calibre, Commitment and Cash.

Let's deal first with the question of calibre. Like any mature candidate who is changing career, your chance of getting a place on a competitive academic course will depend upon your degree class and the quality of your references. The more academic the course, the more importance will be attached to the class of your degree. With a third class degree you are unlikely to be accepted on to a clinical psychology training course, but if you have suitable experience and first-rate references, you may be offered a place on a social work training course where more emphasis is placed on your personal maturity and suitability than on academic achievements.

It is important to remember that just because you have spent a period working as a teacher, it doesn't mean that you can't apply for places on a variety of training schemes for graduates. Sometimes courses may stipulate how recently you must have graduated, but for other courses there is no such requirement. For example, there are currently no fewer than 57 different SERC-funded 'conversion courses' throughout the country. These courses are designed to allow graduates in fields outside new technology to gain a postgraduate qualification (often an MSc) in some aspect of new technology such as computing, information technology or data processing. Some of these conversion courses aim only to 'convert' science or maths graduates, but others are open to graduates of any discipline. I have spoken to the admissions tutors from a number of conversion courses to find out what sort of student they are looking for. They are unanimous in saying that they want bright (but not necessarily recent) graduates, who are numerate and possess the ability to acquire new skills. The admissions tutors aren't *specifically* looking for ex-teachers, but if you have a good degree and can demonstrate that you are of the right calibre, then you have a reasonable chance of getting on the course.

The second C is commitment. I would qualify the 'anything is possible' approach with the proviso 'provided you are really committed'. It's not easy to find yourself listening to lectures, taking notes and, worse still, writing assignments, after possibly many years of giving lectures, dictating notes and giving out assignments yourself. You must make sure that you are sufficiently dedicated before you sign up for a particular training. Having said this, I found the experience of having worked as a teacher greatly assisted me when I went back to studying. As a teacher you have to learn how to organise knowledge and how to write clearly — two skills which are invaluable when the positions are reversed, and the teacher becomes the student.

Finally, you need to consider the question of cash. Whether this is a crucial factor will differ from course to course and from teacher to teacher. The grant position is complex and is discussed below (on pp.111-15). You are more flexible if you can be supported by a partner or parents, but the fees alone can be crippling, to say nothing of living expenses, so do a lot of hard thinking before you embark on a full-time training course without a grant. The section on money also discusses applying to a charitable trust for a grant, but the likelihood of success is remote. As an alternative, in a few careers where you are almost guaranteed a well paid job on completion of the training course (eg a Master of Business Administration), you might be able to arrange a reasonable loan from the bank.

Part-time training courses are available in some career areas, and these have many advantages from the financial point of view. Fees are considerably lower and you can combine the studying with paid work. Remember that as a teacher you can probably earn some money through part-time teaching (which is admittedly quite scarce), supply work or private coaching. Many of the inner-city education authorities are desperate for supply teachers. Although the work is often demoralising it is reasonably lucrative, and can help you finance your way through a part-time course. Supply work also has the advantage that you can drop it when your course becomes particularly demanding, eg near exam time, and then take it up again when there is less pressure. A number of ex-teachers in my sample financed their way through part-time courses (and in a few cases full-time courses, although this is not to be recommended) by taking on some supply work on the side.

Opting for re-training is not an easy step, and this section has shown that there are a number of points that you should consider. Talk through all these points with someone before you make any final decisions. Ensure that you *really* want to work in this new field, and that studying the course will provide you with a reasonable chance of obtaining a job in the area. Ask yourself whether studying will impose an intolerable strain (financially and/or emotionally) on you and your family. Only proceed on the course if you are entirely satisfied with your answers to these questions.

## Sources of information about courses

### 1. Educational Guidance Services for Adults (EGSA)

There are now a number of EGSAs in operation throughout the country. These services aim to provide free information to clients about educational and training opportunities. They are open to adults of any age, and any educational background. It must be mentioned, however, that many services see the thrust of their work as being directed towards those adults who missed out on educational opportunities and they may have little experience in dealing with teachers, all of whom are well qualified. But this does not mean that they won't offer you advice and information about the availability of courses. Moreover, each EGSA is different from the next, so in some areas they will be of more use to the career-changing teacher than in others.

As the service is free, if you have a query about where to find a particular course it would certainly be a good starting point to consult your local EGSA; if they can't help, they may direct you to a suitable book or agency. To find out the address of your nearest service, write to:

ECCTIS
PO Box 88
Walton Hall
Milton Keynes MK7 6DB
*Tel:* 0908 368924

Ask them to send you a free copy of the *Directory of Educational Guidance Services for Adults.*

## 2. Educational Counselling and Credit Transfer Information Service (ECCTIS)

ECCTIS is a national computerised service which provides free information about courses in further and higher education. The ECCTIS data base includes information about all postgraduate taught courses, and all first degree courses throughout the UK. They also have information about certificated courses of more than six weeks full-time or equivalent part-time duration.

*Putting enquiries to ECCTIS*
As the ECCTIS data base is large, any very broad enquiry may produce an unmanageable number of answers. ECCTIS therefore advises its enquirers to specify the following information:

● What subject(s) you want to study
● What level you want to study at
● Preferred mode of study (eg full or part time)
● Preference (if any) about where you want to study in the UK

You can put your enquiries to ECCTIS in a number of different ways:

(a) *Telephone.* Immediate answers will be given over the telephone. If appropriate, more detailed print-out information will be sent by post to enquirers. Telephone 0908 368921. There is also an answerphone available during out-of-office hours.

(b) *Letter.* Write to ECCTIS at the address given on p.95. Make sure that you specify the four items of information about courses listed above.

(c) *Prestel.* Using the ECCTIS gateway available through Prestel 888, you can carry out your own direct on-line search of the data base. Enquiries can be sent to ECCTIS using the response frame on Prestel 21161. When ECCTIS receives the response frame enquiry, the data base is searched, and the relevant print-out information will be sent to you by post.

## 3. Information about all postgraduate courses

The most comprehensive guide to postgraduate courses in the UK is CRAC's *Graduate Studies*, which is an annual publication. It includes brief summaries of all research facilities and postgraduate courses. Professional training courses, eg in social work, or short courses of less than six months, are not covered. For each course included in the guide, the following information is given: brief synopsis, qualification awarded, period of study and entrance requirements.

## 4. Information about CNAA postgraduate and post-experience courses

Write to the Council for National Academic Awards (CNAA) and ask them to send you a free copy of *The Directory of Postgraduate and Post-experience Courses.* This is a *preliminary* guide to courses at postgraduate and post-experience level which have been approved by CNAA. As the CNAA offers courses in a huge range of different subjects, many of which are part time, it is a good idea to send off for this directory to find out what courses are available.

## 5. The associate student scheme

The associate student scheme was initiated by Hatfield Polytechnic, but now many other polytechnics also accept associate students. In the Hatfield scheme mature students study one or more units from within polytechnic degree or diploma programmes, without having to enrol for the whole programme. If you want to gain specialist knowledge in an area, but you haven't time to take on a part-time degree or diploma course, the associate student scheme may be a solution. Associate students are not taught as a separate group; they study alongside students who are taking the whole degree or diploma programme. As an associate student you can choose whether or not to be examined. If you do opt to take the exams, any passes can be credited to you should you subsequently enrol for the corresponding full degree or diploma course.

Attendance may be day or evening, depending on the time of day of the course you are interested in. You can expect to attend two to three hours a week for every course unit studied. If you are interested in finding out more about this scheme, write to:

The Academic Registrar
The Hatfield Polytechnic
PO Box 109
Hatfield
Hertfordshire AL10 9AB

Ask to be sent a copy of the *Associate Student Handbook.*
Other polytechnics also offer the scheme. If a course at your local

polytechnic sounds interesting, but you could only manage one or two units at a time, contact the course tutor and ask if they will accept you as an associate student.

## 6. Educational and training provision outside the state sector

To find out about opportunities outside the state sector, consult a directory called DITTO *(Directory of Independent Training and Tutorial Organisations)*, by Elizabeth Summerson and Maureen Davies. It was published in 1985 by Careers Consultants Ltd.

The directory includes courses in a broad range of subjects, eg accountancy, law, hotel and catering, beauty therapy, psychotherapy. Details of correspondence and home study courses are also provided, and there is information on how to finance yourself. It is made clear that inclusion in the guide does not guarantee that the course is of a high standard, but useful guidelines for checking the quality of the course are suggested.

## 7. Adult education and training opportunities

Consult *Second Chances*, an annual guide published by the National Extension College.

This book is intended for anyone wanting to further their education or training in any way, and it covers the whole range of provision, eg training for self-employment, learning by post, evening classes and university and polytechnic courses. It is an extremely useful reference source.

## 8. Training opportunities in new technology

Many of the ex-teachers interviewed for this research went into some branch of computing. They had a variety of jobs within the computing field, eg graphic designer using computer graphics, writer of computer manuals, training consultant with a software company, and computer programmer. At a time when opportunities in many areas are contracting, there is still a need for bright graduates to enter the field of computing. Moreover, you don't have to work for a computer company to get a job in computing. New technology is being introduced right across the board, in the service and manufacturing industries and in the professions. In all these areas there is a great need for computer-literate personnel who can train other staff in the use of computers. If you get basic (or even high level) training in computing, you can combine this specialised knowledge with your teaching experience, and find yourself a job training others.

*The Directory of Opportunities in New Technology* (1985), published by Kogan Page, is a basic guide to postgraduate training courses and to companies taking on graduate trainees in the fields of computer programming, electrical and electronic engineering, telecommunications and engineering. If you are under 30 and have a good degree in a relevant science subject, you should have no difficulty in finding yourself a company that will offer you a traineeship. But the guide also gives information about some companies that are willing to take on graduate trainees who do not have a degree in a relevant science subject, although it will be harder to get accepted if you do not have any sort of science background. To do yourself justice on your application form, remember to mention any computing experience that you have had from teaching. If you've used microcomputers as part of your teaching (eg in biology), attended a computing course at the local teachers' centre, or devised the timetable on the school computer, then say so! This is all evidence of your ability to use computers and could help you to get accepted.

In addition to company training schemes there are numerous other courses on offer: everything from full-time taught postgraduate degrees to 10-week MSC-funded courses and from OU home study packages to evening classes at your local adult education centre.

*Choosing an appropriate course*
Deciding which course is appropriate is not always easy. In *Equal Opportunities: A Career Guide* (1984) by Ruth Miler and Anna Alston, published by Penguin, there is a very clear, brief account of the different types of job available in the computing field and the sort of training that you need for these jobs. Another useful book is *Working with computers* available from the Women's Computer Centre. This book gives a description of the different types of jobs in the computing field as well as information about training courses and how to find a job. The Centre also produces a list of women-only computer courses. For further details about the work of the organisation, contact:

The Women's Computer Centre
Wesley House
Wild Court
London WC2
*Tel:* 01-430 0112

The British Computer Society publishes a useful free booklet on careers in computing (for address see below) and although it is intended for school-leavers it may help you decide what training you need. You can also contact the society directly and check with them whether the course you are considering will actually help you to get employment in your career of interest. Their address is:

The British Computer Society
13 Mansfield Street
London W1M 0BD
*Tel:* 01-637 0471

In the sections below I consider courses across the whole spectrum, from the most basic ones that assume no prior knowledge or special aptitude, to advanced postgraduate degrees.

*Scientific and Economic Research Council
(SERC)-funded provision*
*(a) Conversion courses* are designed to enable graduates from non-technical, and sometimes even non-scientific backgrounds to acquire skills in the field of information technology. On most of the courses graduates will be expected to have some computing experience, but in a few there is a special introductory course which brings students up to the required standard. Clearly, the less computing experience you have, the more the admissions tutors will expect evidence of great commitment and exceptional ability. If you are interested in a course that requires some background, phone up the course tutor and ask what they consider to be suitable experience. Perhaps taking an OU computer course (see p.102) or enrolling as an associate student at your local polytechnic will give you the pre-course experience that you need.

A number of places on each of the conversion courses receive SERC funding. If you are awarded a studentship your fees will be paid and you will receive a maintenance grant. For a list of all the courses which have SERC studentships, write to:

SERC
Polaris House
North Star Avenue
Swindon SN2 1ET
*Tel:* 0793 2622

The list provided by the SERC does not contain course details; you therefore have to contact each of the course organisers separately to obtain further information. The actual studentships are advertised in the *Guardian*.

*(b) The Teaching Company Scheme* is designed to increase the collaboration between industry and academics, in order to raise industrial performance. This SERC-funded scheme sets up teaching company programmes in which a polytechnic or university takes part in a company project to achieve a substantial change in a designated area of the company's operations.

In order to carry out the scheme, the permanent academic staff are assisted by high-calibre graduates who have been recruited on two-year teaching company associateships. Becoming an associate offers an opportunity to gain both industrial experience and academic knowledge in the field of new technology. The associates are based full time at the company, working in collaboration with company and academic staff, and they receive a salary rather than a student grant. The associates also receive further tuition at the university or polytechnic, and many register for a higher degree.

In notes sent out by the SERC they state that 'associates should be between 21 and 28 with a good honours degree in engineering or the physical sciences'.

If you fit into this category and you decide to apply, remember to discuss the relevance of your teaching experience at an interview. For example, teaching associates need to be able to work with the other members of the academic and company team, to produce clear written material and to have sufficient initiative to get on with their own work without continual supervision. These are three skills that experienced teachers have acquired.

Vacancies for associates are advertised in the *Guardian*. In addition, you can write directly to the SERC at the address given above, and they will send you a list of teaching company schemes that are currently recruiting associates.

*Manpower Services Commission (MSC) provision*
Working out what MSC courses are available, when, where, and who is eligible, can be quite a tricky task. To complicate the issue further, the different schemes keep on changing their names (eg TOPS has been relaunched as JTS—Job Training Scheme) which makes it even harder to keep track of what is going on.

Training courses in the field of new technology which are likely to be of interest to the career-changing teacher are as follows:

*(a) The Job Training Scheme (JTS).* Under this scheme there is a variety of courses available including those in the field of new

ᴜᴄᴄhnology (eg computer programming, information processing) and also in other areas such as personnel and sales management. The courses generally last three to six months, but a few last up to a year, and may even result in an academic qualification. Most but not all courses are full time. The MSC pays the course fees, and for most full-time courses you are also given a maintenance allowance.

Some courses are particularly appropriate for teachers and allow you to build on your teaching experience, eg a course which trains people to design computer-based learning materials. Many of the ex-teachers in the sample who had gone into computing obtained their basic training on a JTS (or TOPS, as it used to be called) course.

The MSC lays down the following criteria regarding eligibility:

- You are unemployed, about to become unemployed, or are prepared to give up your job (ie if you are employed while applying for a place on the course, but are prepared to hand in your notice if you are awarded a place, you are eligible)
- You have been away from full-time education for a total of two years
- You intend to work in a job which uses your course skills

Some JTS courses are advertised in the national press, eg the *Guardian* and in PER's *Executive Post*. In order to find out about JTS courses that are operating in your area, you can also contact your local Jobcentre (the address and telephone number are given in the telephone directory under Manpower Services Commission).

*(b) Access to Information Technology Courses* provide a very basic low level introduction to computing and information technology rather than training you for a job in the field. They are suitable for people who have never before been in the same room as a computer or word processor, and they give you an opportunity of getting 'hands on' experience. The courses are usually held in the evenings or at weekends, so you can enrol if you are in full-time employment. The cost is low (50p an hour, or free for the unemployed) and the courses tend to take an evening a week for about 10 weeks. A list of courses is available from your local Jobcentre.

*Home study courses*
*(a) The Open University*, as part of its continuing education programme, offers a number of computing courses, eg there is a course entitled 'Computing and Computers' which provides a general introduction to computer science, and assumes no previous know-

ledge of the field. The course covers programming in PASCAL, the study of data structures, systems analysis and systems design.

Further details of this and other courses can be obtained from:

> The Open University
> Walton Hall
> Milton Keynes MK7 6AA

*(b)  The National Extension College* offers an introductory course in computer programming, '30-hour BASIC'. This covers programming in BASIC, but special editions of the course are also available for ZX81, Spectrum, Electron and Oric computers. In addition, NEC offers more advanced course on BASIC programming.

The material in the introductory course covers the syllabus of the City and Guilds Certificate in computer literacy, but it can be taken as a non-exam course if you wish. No prior knowledge of computers is assumed. For further details write to:

> The National Extension College
> 18 Brooklands Avenue
> Cambridge CB2 2HN
> *Tel:* 0223 316644

*(c)  The Directory of Independent Training and Tutorial Organisations* gives details of other organisations offering home-study computer courses. See p.98 for information about this directory.

*Adult education classes*
These classes, run by the local education authority, offer enormous scope for developing computer skills. As many classes are offered in the evening, they can be combined with full-time employment. *Floodlight*, the directory of part-time adult education in Inner London, lists over 200 different courses in computer programming; everything from O level standard to postgraduate diplomas! The provision is most extensive in London, but it is likely that you will be able to find a suitable part-time adult education class in most parts of the country.

To find out about courses, ask for the prospectus of your local adult education institute at the public library.

## 9.  Training courses in management

There are three preliminary points that must be made.

1. Management is not a uniform activity. You could bring together ten people who call themselves 'managers' and find that

there was no similarity between them in what they actually do at work, or what they earn. This point is clearly made by Ruth Miller and Anna Alston, in *Equal Opportunities: A Career Guide* (1984) published by Penguin:

> Management is a vast and confusing field, with vague terminology. It is not a career in the usual sense, but an activity, the purpose of which is to make the best use of available resources—human, money, material, equipment—in order to achieve a given objective.

2. You may think that if you want to leave teaching to go into management in industry, you should be applying for the post of 'general manager'. But this shows a misunderstanding of management functions. The general manager is not a low-level manager gaining 'general' experience but a senior employee who is responsible for co-ordinating the work of several different departments, and probably just below board level.

Managers don't start off as 'general managers'; instead they specialise in a particular function, eg marketing, distribution or purchasing and supply. A corollary of this is that the type of training you need depends upon the area of management you intend to pursue. A personnel manager requires a different training from someone hoping to go into marketing.

3. You don't have to have the word 'manager' in your job description to have acquired managerial experience. If as a teacher you have been head of department or head of house, you have had managerial responsibility. These posts involve leading a team of teachers, deciding and implementing policy, and reporting to a higher committee. Having responsibility for resources, curriculum development or school-community links is also managerial experience. Many teachers have been managers for years without realising it.

## Choosing your field

Before you can find yourself a suitable training programme you need to decide what *sort* of manager you want to be. For example, if you haven't yet made up your mind whether you want to go into production or marketing, you cannot make any further decisions about your training.

Chapters 2 and 3 give detailed information about deciding what to do next and how to find out more about jobs in your chosen field. It is worth mentioning that there are AGCAS booklets (see p.30) on many areas of management, eg marketing and production. These booklets provide a good starting point for your reading.

## What next?

Most management training is 'on the job', provided by the company or organisation. It is the opposite of a career such as law. To become a lawyer it is a question of study first, practise later. With jobs in management your best bet is to get taken on by a company providing management traineeships in the particular speciality that interests you. In this way you combine actual work experience with the training given by the company.

Once you have been accepted as a management trainee and worked for a year or two, you can improve your prospects by studying for a further professional qualification (eg the Diploma in Management Studies) during the evenings or on a day-release basis. If you would be willing to do some further studying after you have worked for a year or so, then make it clear on your application form and at interviews. As an applicant who knows what further professional qualifications are needed, and who is willing to devote time to studying, you demonstrate the extent of your commitment to a potential employer.

## If you are under 30

If you are under 30 and want to pursue a career in management, try to get a company to take you on as a graduate management trainee. This won't necessarily be quick or simple to achieve. It will be easier for graduates who studied engineering, technological subjects, computing or business studies. But console yourself with the knowledge that about one-third of the vacancies for management trainee schemes are for 'any discipline' graduates, including those with a BEd.

Don't expect to be taken on by the first company: you may have to put up with a number of failed application forms and interviews before you finally get accepted. A lot will depend on how you present yourself. Convince the employer that as a teacher you have had managerial experience, and you are used to working extremely hard under stressful conditions.

The prospective employer is likely to have a number of qualms about employing you. Do you know what management outside education entails? Is changing career something of a whim on your part, or are you truly committed to change? Have you the ability to learn and adapt to your new career?

One way of dispelling a potential employer's doubts would be to take a course in management education. If you studied in the evening or at home you could combine the course with teaching, although this would be very hard work. A possibility to consider is the Diploma in Management run by the Open University. This provides you with an excellent theoretical grounding to help you switch from management in education to management in industry or the public sector. By successfully completing the course you would demonstrate to the employer that you *do* know what management in industry entails, that your career change is not merely a whim, and that you have the capacity to learn.

One drawback of the OU course must be mentioned. Although the British Institute of Management think highly of the course, many employers haven't heard of its existence. But if you are willing to stand up for the course, and tell employers what you gained from taking it, then studying for the Diploma provides one way of helping you get accepted on to a management traineeship scheme.

For further details, write to:

> The Open Business School
> The Open University
> PO Box 76
> Milton Keynes MK7 6AN
> *Tel:* 0908 653473

You can also write to the British Institute of Management who will provide you with a list of other management courses that can be studied by distance learning. Their address is:

> The British Institute of Management
> Management House
> Cottingham Road
> Corby
> Northants NN17 1TT
> *Tel:* 0536 204222

### How to find out about vacancies

Some management trainee posts are advertised in national newspapers such as the *Guardian*. In addition, you can find out which companies take on graduates in your field of interest, and your geographical area, by consulting the three graduate directories: *Graduate Employment and Training, Directory of Opportunities for Graduates* and *Graduate Opportunities*. See p.48, Chapter 3, for further details about these publications.

These directories will probably give you the names of many companies to which you could apply. An important point to remember is that your chances of success are greater if you apply to smaller and middle-sized companies, rather than to the major 'household name' organisations.

## If you are over 30

If you are over 30, breaking into management is harder, as it is unlikely that you will be accepted on a graduate traineeship scheme. And unfortunately you will not be considered for management posts that ask for someone aged between 30 and 40, as you have not got 10-15 years of company management experience behind you.

However, older teachers *do* succeed in moving into management. If you have had a successful career as a teacher, involving considerable management experience, then with great persistence, you will be able to persuade a company to train you in some managerial function notwithstanding your age. Writing a large number of letters to companies listed in the directories and doing a first-rate advertising campaign on yourself should eventually yield a job offer. If you have been in charge of school-industry links or have taken part in the TVEI programme you will be in a stronger position, as an employer can see that you have an understanding of, and links with industry.

An easier step for the older teacher is to move into educational administration. As a starting point you would need to have had managerial responsibility in school. In addition, you should also consider taking a course in education management or educational administration. The DES booklet *Long courses for Teachers* (see p.110) gives details of relevant courses. Having made the move into educational administration and gained experience in that sphere, you could then apply for other managerial posts in public administration or, if you prefer, in the private sector.

## The Master of Business Administration (MBA) course

When you hear the three letters MBA, names like Harvard or London Business School immediately spring to mind. But the British Institute of Management's list of postgraduate management courses contains no fewer than 25 different universities and polytechnics in the UK which provide the MBA course—many on a part-time basis. Furthermore, Strathclyde Business School and Warwick University offer distance-learning MBA courses.

In reality, employers often have a distinct hierarchy of preference, for example placing London/Manchester/Cranfield MBAs at the top and some of the newer polytechnic courses at the bottom.

This is *not* to say that the polytechnic courses don't provide an excellent management education, only that these MBAs are less prestigious.

MBA course tutors are not looking for graduates who are still wet behind the ears—instead they like their students to have had at least three years' work experience. Although most MBA students come from management in industry or the public sector, your background in education does not make you ineligible for the course. The primary concern of the course tutors is to choose candidates who are high achievers at work, and they may be quite flexible about the type of work experience you have had.

The Business Schools, then, don't want 21-year old graduates, but equally they don't want you to be too old. The London Business School states that 'we expect most of our MBA participants to be in their mid-20s to mid-30s', and you are unlikely to be accepted on to one of the major university MBA programmes if you are older than this. In addition, the most prestigious courses only accept students of a certain academic standard who have a good first degree and high scores on the Graduate Management Admissions Test. The latter test (also known as GMAT) is designed to test the candidate's ability for clear and systematic thought, and it is *extremely* rigorous and demanding.

The final problem is money. Fees on the prestigious MBA programmes are high. For example, in 1985-86 fees for the London Business School full-time MBA course were £1632 per annum, and the course duration is 21 months. Some students will obtain grants, and others may be able to arrange bank loans at reasonable rates of interest. If you are accepted for a place on a Business Graduates Association approved MBA course, then you may be able to obtain a loan with the scheme that they operate. Further details are available from:

> The Business Graduates Association
> 28 Margaret Street
> London W1
> *Tel:* 01-637 7611

Studying for an MBA at one of the top business schools will only be appropriate for a few teachers. You will have to be under 35, extremely bright, and be able to afford the fees. Having said this, on completion of the course you stand an excellent chance of getting an extremely lucrative high-powered managerial job. For example, the Business Graduates Association has estimated that the average increase in salary between starting and finishing one of their MBA courses is 67 per cent.

Entry requirements for some of the university and polytechnic courses will be less stringent than those described above, fees are lower, and they may be more flexible on the question of age. But these courses don't guarantee you a high-paid managerial job in the same way.

To conclude, if you really want to switch from teaching to management, and you get a place on a top MBA course, then do it. It will undoubtedly provide the speediest entrance into highly paid managerial positions. However, if you are under 30 and you get accepted on to one of the less well known programmes, think very seriously before you embark on the course straight from teaching. It might be better to apply for a graduate trainee post (which you should get, if you were of sufficient calibre to be accepted on to an MBA course) and then embark on the MBA course a few years later, once you have gained some industrial experience. The company trainee scheme will give you as good, if not better job prospects than a second tier MBA course alone, and you would also get more out of an MBA course once you had some experience of management in industry.

If you are an older teacher with no industrial experience you are unlikely to be accepted on to one of the most prestigious courses. Even if you get a place on one of the other MBA programmes, it would be a risky move to make straight from teaching. To the prospective employer, someone of 35+ who has no industrial experience, but who knows it all in theory, does not seem an attractive proposition. The older teacher would be advised to follow the strategies suggested earlier in this section rather than opting for an MBA course.

## Building on your teaching skills

Not all teachers who read this book are going to decide that they actually want to leave the profession. After working through the self-awareness component of Chapter 2, and perhaps having some career counselling, some teachers will decide that they want to stay in teaching after all. But they will be in a much stronger position knowing that they are staying in teaching because that is what they *want* to do, rather than feeling that perhaps they should be doing something else, if only they knew what!

If you have decided that you want to remain in the profession, there are still important training opportunities for you to pursue.

You could consider further developing some aspect of your specialist subject, eg a maths teacher might want to take an advanced diploma in maths education, in order to increase her chances of becoming a head of department. Or you may want to develop skills in areas such as counselling or educational administration.

The DES and the Welsh Office Education Department publish a booklet called *Long Courses for Teachers Organised by Universities, Polytechnics and Colleges*. This publication contains details of most of the full- and part-time courses in England and Wales which are of special interest to teachers, eg courses in counselling, administration, health education, etc. Information about DES short courses (those of 3-14 days' duration) is not included. Your local teachers' centre, and some public libraries with a good careers section, will have a copy of this booklet.

To find out about the availability of courses in Scotland write to:

The Scottish Education Department
43 Jeffrey Street
Edinburgh EH1 1DN

In addition to universities, polytechnics and colleges, the Open University also has extensive provision in the field of professional development in education.

You can study for an advanced diploma in the following areas: educational management, curriculum and teaching, maths education, post-compulsory education and special needs in education. There is also an MSc course in advanced educational and social research methods. All of these courses are poolable, so that LEAs can reclaim 100 per cent of fees and travel costs incurred by teachers sponsored by them. So you have a fair chance of receiving some funding from your LEA.

As well as the courses listed above, the OU also offers a range of study packs. These are smaller free-standing units dealing with particular topics. Unlike the courses, with a study pack there is no tuition or certification. Study pack topics include: micros in schools, curriculum review and development, youth services projects and maths education. Further details are available from:

ASCO
The Open University
PO Box 76
Milton Keynes MK7 6AN

## Money

Awards for postgraduate training (with a few exceptions, such as the PGCE) are not mandatory. Competition for funding is intense. For most courses you need a certain class of degree to obtain a grant; advanced course studentships and one-year taught courses for a higher degree stipulate at least a second class honours degree, while three-year research studentships require a II-I or above. But just because you have a II-I or a first, you won't necessarily receive an award. All it means is that you are eligible to apply for funding. The final outcome will depend on the particular course you are applying for, the calibre of the other applicants, and the quality of your references.

In most, but not all cases, you don't apply directly to the award-making body, eg the Scientific and Engineering Research Council (SERC). Instead, you apply for a place on the course/research programme that interests you. When you have been accepted, the application for an award is made by the institution offering you a place, rather than by you. Begin by contacting the admissions tutor in the institution where you have applied, and find out how most people on the course/research programme fund themselves. Find out if you have to apply directly to one of the award-making bodies, and if so, to which of the different research councils you should send your application.

Most of the different award-making bodies publish booklets detailing the awards that they provide. The addresses are given in the table on pp.112-13.

## Local education authorities

In general LEAs do not provide grants for postgraduate courses. However, some LEAs will consider giving you a grant for the following courses:

- Accountancy (full-time conversion course only)
- Careers advisory work
- Educational psychology
- Law (final course only)
- Music and drama course for performers
- Ordination course
- Secretarial work
- Youth and community work

| Name of award-making body | Subjects covered | Name of publication | Address |
|---|---|---|---|
| Agriculture and Food Research Council (AFRC) | Agriculture and related topics, food sciences and related topics | (a) *The Regulations Governing Postgraduate Awards*<br>(b) *The Regulations Governing Postgraduate Awards in Food* | 160 Great Portland Street<br>London W1N 6DT |
| Department of Education and Science (DES) | Arts/humanities | (a) *Postgraduate awards 1 – Business*<br>(b) *Postgraduate awards 2 – Studentships*<br>(c) *Postgraduate awards 3 – Information science* | Honeypot Lane<br>Stanmore<br>Middlesex HA7 1AZ |
| Department of Health and Social Security (DHSS) | Social work, paramedical | — | Alexander Fleming House<br>Elephant and Castle<br>London SE1 6BY |
| Economic and Social Research Council (ESRC) | Social services | (a) *ESRC Studentship Handbook*<br>(b) *ESRC Bursary Handbook* | 160 Great Portland Street<br>London W1N 6BA |

| Name of award-making body | Subjects covered | Name of publication | Address |
|---|---|---|---|
| Medical Research Council (MRC) | Medical and related biological sciences | — | 20 Park Crescent London W1N 4AL |
| Ministry of Agriculture Fisheries and Food (MAFF) | Agriculture, food science and related topics | — | Great Westminster House (Room 116) Horseferry Road London SW1P 2AE |
| National Environment Research Council (NERC) | Scientific study of the earth, sea, water and atmosphere | *NERC Training Awards* | Polaris House North Star Avenue Swindon SN2 1EU |
| Science and Engineering Research Council (SERC) | Science and technology not covered by the other research councils | *SERC Studentships and Fellowships* | Secretary's Department (PTSS) Polaris House North Star Avenue Swindon SN2 1ET |

If you are considering any of the above courses, it is always worth applying to your LEA, to see if they are willing to provide you with a grant.

## Students from Scotland and Northern Ireland

For information about postgraduate awards for Scottish students, contact:

> Scottish Education Department—Awards Branch
> Haymarket House
> Clifton Terrace
> Edinburgh EH12 5DR

Students from Northern Ireland should contact:

> Department of Education
> Rathgael House
> Balloo Road
> Bangor
> County Down BT19 2PR
> Northern Ireland

## Educational charities

A few students obtain financial support from educational charities each year. It is worth applying, but you must realise that all these charities receive many more applications than they can possibly support. For further information, look at the following directories in your reference library:

*Educational Charities: A Guide to Educational Trust Funds* (National Union of Students)

*The Directory of Grant Making Trusts* (Charities Aid Foundation)

*The Grants Register* (Macmillan Press)

## Further information

*Consult*

1. The careers advisory service of the polytechnic/university/ college from which you graduated.
2. Your local Educational Guidance Services for Adults; see p.95 for details.

*Read*

1. The AGCAS booklet *Postgraduate Research and Training*. For availability of AGCAS publications see pp.30-31.
2. *Directory of Opportunities for Graduates*, Vol.4, published annually by New Opportunity Press (now Newpoint).
3. CRAC's *Students' Guide to Graduate Studies*.

## Career Development Loans

In certain parts of the country the MSC now runs a scheme for Career Development Loans. This pilot scheme applies to anyone over 18 living in, or intending to train in, Aberdeen, Bristol/Bath, Greater Manchester and Reading/Slough.

Under the scheme the banks will consider lending you money for a vocational training course of your choice if it lasts for at least one week, and no more than one year. The training course must significantly improve your career and employment prospects: a training course in computing might be accepted, but one in the study of medieval embroidery certainly would not.

When you have obtained a place on a suitable course you apply to one of the banks involved in the scheme for a loan. If your application is successful, you get an interest-free loan for the duration of the training course and for up to three months afterwards.

This scheme is being piloted from April 1986 for a three-year period. A leaflet and further information are available from Jobcentres in the pilot areas.

## Self-employment

A number of the ex-teachers in my sample have become self-employed. In some cases the connection between their teaching experience and their self-employment is clear cut, eg the woodwork teacher who has become a self-employed carpenter, the home economics teacher who runs her own catering business, the art teacher who works as a graphic designer, and the music teacher who set up her own music shop. In other cases the ex-teachers use skills that they had originally developed as hobbies and have turned these into their business idea, eg the primary teacher who has set up a knitwear design company, and the deputy head who has started a house-decorating firm.

If you are contemplating starting your own business, loss of financial security is probably your biggest concern. But in the early days of your business it may be possible for you to combine self-employment with some part-time or supply teaching in order to guarantee a small but steady income. The knitwear designer and graphic designer mentioned above both taught for one day a week in order to have some minimal sense of financial security.

A detailed discussion of the relative advantages and disadvantages of self-employment is beyond the scope of this book. If you have a marketable idea and you are considering setting up your own business, you should begin by doing some reading on the subject. The following guides are particularly recommended: *The Small Business Action Kit* (1986), by John Rosthorn *et al.*, published by Kogan Page, and *Starting Your Own Business*, published by the Consumers' Association.

## Training courses on self-employment

Like the field of computing, there is no shortage of courses in starting up your own business, and the problem is deciding which is most appropriate. The list below gives an outline of the different sorts of courses on offer. It is also worth consulting your local adult education centre to see if they provide suitable courses.

### 1.  Home-study courses

*(a)  The National Extension College* runs a 'small business course'. It is introductory, and aims to help you decide if self-employment is for you, and to assess the viability of your business idea. Basic practical advice on finance, taxation and marketing is also given. Further details are available from:

> The National Extension College
> 18 Brooklands Avenue
> Cambridge CB2 2HN

*(b)  The Open University* offers a course called 'Start up your own business', developed by the OU Business School. It is directed at anyone who is interested in setting up a business, and aims to get them off on the right footing. The course material is divided into four main sections: planning; reviewing the industry; preparing to run your business; and alternatives.

This course is at a higher level than the NEC one mentioned above. A special feature of the OU course is that it includes close contact with a personal adviser for up to nine months. The culmination of the course is the presentation of your business plan to a panel of experts who assess its feasibility. A few sponsorship places on this course are available. If you are seriously considering self-employment but have doubts about the feasibility of your idea, you would be well advised to take this OU course. Further details can be obtained from the Startup Project Officer, OU Business School, at the OU address given on p.106.

*2. Manpower Services Commission provision*
*(a) The Training for Enterprise Programme* includes training provision for people starting up their own business. There are different courses available, depending upon the size of enterprise you are contemplating, and the courses may be full or part time. Unemployed, self-employed and employed people aged over 18 are all eligible. Further information is available from your local MSC Training Division Office.

*(b) The Graduate Enterprise Programme* (GEP) is designed to help recent graduates develop their own business idea and then set up a business. It is partly sponsored by the MSC as well as by many large commercial concerns such as the clearing banks. GEP provides a comprehensive package of support lasting 18 months and consists of a period of training based at a business school, business counselling, follow-up help and financial assistance.

The MSC provides you with a training allowance to cover the residential period spent at the business school. It may also provide a market research budget of up to £1200 to help you during the non-residential periods. In addition, you may be eligible for an MSC Enterprise Allowance once you actually get your business started.

To be considered for a place on the scheme you need to have an excellent business idea that you want to develop, but there is also the question of how recently you graduated. The main purpose of the scheme is to get *recent* graduates to set up their own business. If you haven't been away from full-time education (eg a BEd or a PGCE course) for more than two years, you are definitely eligible to apply for a place on the scheme. After that the position becomes somewhat hazy. In theory the two-year rule applies, but in practice if you left full-time education three or four years ago and you have a *fantastic* idea, then with great perseverance, you might argue your way into the scheme. It is worth noting that the Northern Ireland programme, in an attempt to encourage business development in the province, does not impose this recency of graduation restriction.

There are three schemes operating within the English Graduate Enterprise Programme, based at Cranfield Institute of Technology, Durham University and Warwick University. The English

GEP is coordinated from Cranfield and further information is available from:

Michelle Kent
Programme Administrator—Graduate Enterprise Programme
Cranfield School of Management
Cranfield Institute of Technology
Cranfield
Bedford MK43 0AL
*Tel:* 0234 751122

Scotland, Wales and Northern Ireland have their own schemes, and the addresses are as follows:

Scottish Enterprise Foundation
University of Stirling
Stirling FK9 4LA
Scotland
*Tel:* 0786 73171

Graduate Enterprise in Wales
St Davids University College
University of Wales
Lampeter
Dyfed SA48 7ED
*Tel:* 0570 422351

Graduate Enterprise Programme—Northern Ireland
The Northern Ireland Small Business Institute
University of Ulster
Jordanstown
Co Antrim BT37 0QB
*Tel:* 0232 365131

**Other sources of help**

*The Small Firms Service* provides free information to help you solve a wide variety of business problems, and also offers a business counselling service staffed by experienced personnel. You can find out the address of your local Small Firms Service by dialling 100 and asking for Freefone Enterprise.

*Council for Small Industries in Rural Areas (CoSIRA)* offers free information and advice to people thinking of setting up a business in an English rural area. For information about the work of the organisation, write to:

CoSIRA Information Section
141 Castle Street
Salisbury
Wiltshire SP1 3TP
*Tel:* 0722 336255

*Local enterprise agencies* can offer a wide range of support and advice to people setting up a business. To find your local enterprise agency, contact:

England:   Business in the Community
           227a City Road
           London EC1 1JU
           *Tel:* 01-253 3716

Scotland:  Scottish Business in the Community
           Eagle Star House
           25 St Andrews Square
           Edinburgh
           *Tel:* 031-556 9761

*The Cooperative Development Agency* provides advice and information to help you set up a cooperative organisation. Their address is:

Broadmead House
21 Panton Street
London SW1Y 4DR
*Tel:* 01-839 2988

## Chapter 7
# Finale

This was the final question that I put to my sample of ex-teachers:

> 'What advice would you give someone who is considering leaving the profession?'

As a conclusion I would like to record some of their replies.

> Do it! Make as many enquiries as possible. Explore every avenue. But don't do it on impulse. I don't have any regrets.

> If you really want to, don't just talk about it—do it!

> Explore other avenues, even if you only have slight misgivings about teaching. If you don't, you will only develop more and more frustration and resentment. If you decide to stay in teaching, you will have the reassurance that your decision to stay is a positive one.

> Ensure that when you are deciding to leave it is because of teaching itself, and not that you are unhappy in your particular school. Don't rush into another career—find out as much as you can about possible options. Consider which are your personal talents and in which job you would be able to use them. Think about what you want from your work.

> Do it! Decide on an area, get some background information, and keep a look-out. It may take time to get the job you want, but it is well worth the time and effort.

> If you want to leave you should... Easier said than done, but demoralised teachers are bad teachers. As a teacher you have loads of accumulated skills that are applicable to industry or commerce.

> Don't be brow-beaten into believing that teaching is no preparation for other jobs—on the contrary, it is excellent experience. It gives you all sorts of useful skills especially the all-important communication skills. Don't think it's too late to change—it's never too late!

# Appendices

## Appendix 1
# Sources of Information

*British Qualifications* (1986), Kogan Page. Detailed guide to all qualifications in Britain. It may be useful for deciphering the qualifications of the people who are interviewing you.

*Current British Directories* lists all the directories published for the UK and Commonwealth, so you can find out about specific trade/professional directories. Published by CBD Research, who also offer: *Directory of British Associations* which lists all trade and professional associations.

*Dun & Bradstreet's British Middle Market Directory.* Information on smaller British companies.

*Dun & Bradstreet's Guide to Key British Enterprises.* Basic information on several thousand British companies.

*Dun & Bradstreet's International Market Guide.* Information on companies in many parts of the world.

*Extel Statistical Services* supply up-to-date information on individual companies. For each company, the information is held on a card, and the cards are available in many public reference libraries. Alternatively they can be supplied from:

> Extel Statistical Services
> 37-45 Paul Street
> London EC2A 4PB

The cost is £2.60 for a company quoted on the London Stock Exchange and £7.80 for any other company. There is also a European Extel Service covering some quoted European companies.

*The Financial Times Microfilm Record.* Monthly index of all the subjects/information contained in that month's issues of the FT. This will enable you to find out very up-to-date information.

*The Kompass Directory (UK).* Entries on over 28 000 firms giving details of the firms' trading activities.

*The International Kompass Directory.* As above, by country, to cover the international market.

*Standard and Poor's Corporation Research.* Information on the 6000 largest firms in the US.

*The Stock Exchange Year Book.* Brief report on all quoted public companies. Foreign stock exchange year books are also available.

*The Times 1000.* Information on the top 1000 companies, given in ranked order of size.

*Who Owns Whom.* An index of parent companies, their subsidiaries and associates. A continental edition is also available.

*Who's Who.* Brief autobiographies of prominent people. May prove useful for finding out about the senior personnel in the organisation.

## Additional points

1. In-depth surveys of particular industries/markets are often undertaken by national newspapers. The librarian in the public reference library may be able to tell you if there are any recent surveys of relevance.

2. Companies House
   55 City Road
   London EC1Y 1BB
   Contains detailed information about all UK companies. There are offices in Belfast and Edinburgh too. Going directly to them may be the only way to find out financial information about private UK companies. Postal enquiries are dealt with at:

   > Companies House
   > Crown Way
   > Maindy
   > Cardiff CF4 3UZ
   > *Tel:* 0222 388588

   A charge is made for use of the service.

## Specialist libraries

1. The City Business Library
   Gillett House
   55 Basinghall Street
   London EC2V 5BX
   *Tel:* 01-638 8215

Contains a mass of information on UK-based companies and other organisations.

2. The Science Reference Library
   25 Southampton Buildings
   Chancery Lane
   London WC2A 1AW
   *Tel:* 01-468 8721

   This library produces a series of guides called 'Aids to readers', and Guide Number 28, *Business Literature and the Science Reference Library*, gives the categories under which business information is catalogued eg Trade/Business Journals, Industry Surveys and Market Research Reports.

## Appendix 2
# Your Pension

If you have been teaching for less than five years, you are entitled to a refund of your contributions to the Teachers' Superannuation Scheme (from 6 April 1988 this period will be shortened to two years).

If you have been teaching for more than five years, you have three alternatives:

1. You can leave your contributions in the Teachers' Superannuation Scheme which will pay you a 'preserved' pension on your retirement.
2. You can transfer the value of your contributions to your new employer's scheme, if your new employer offers such a scheme.
3. You can transfer the value of your contributions to a single premium pension policy known as a 'Section 32 Buy-Out' or a 'Buy-Out Bond'.

   Among the leading insurance companies offering this contract are:

   > Equitable Life
   > Equity Law
   > National Provident Institution
   > Norwich Union
   > Scottish Equitable
   > Scottish Mutual
   > Scottish Widows
   > Standard Life

   If you contact one of these companies they will send you a questionnaire asking for details of your contributions to the Teachers' Superannuation Scheme. You should send this on to the DES in Darlington who should supply you with the necessary information. Once you have returned the completed questionnaire to the insurance company, they will send you a quotation which you can then compare with the other alternatives.

What you *cannot* do, however, if you have been teaching for more than five years, is obtain a refund of your contributions. You will not receive any pension benefits from former employment until you reach retirement age, unless you are subsequently forced to retire early through ill-health.

Before you can make any decisions about your pension arrangements, you must write to:

> The Pensions Branch
> Department of Education and Science
> Mowden Hall
> Staindrop Road
> Darlington
> County Durham BD3 9BG

quoting your

> full name
> date of birth
> address
> DES number
> National Insurance number
> Number of years of teaching service

You should ask the Pensions Branch:

1. To give you a detailed explanation of your entitlement to a 'preserved pension'.

2. To quote a transfer value to your new employer's scheme.

3. To quote a transfer value to a Section 32 Buy-Out Bond.

It may take them several weeks, or even months to reply, but do not give up. Keep copies of every letter you write to them and be persistent.

Obtaining accurate information and making the right decision could make a substantial difference to your final pension.

If you think you need expert advice to help you decide which of the three alternatives outlined above would be best for your individual case, then you should first of all get in touch with the Pensions Department of your new company. Alternatively, you could entrust the research to a reputable insurance broker.

You may find it time-consuming to research the different alternatives, but rest assured that it will be time well spent. You will have taken an important step towards securing a financially comfortable retirement.

# Index